RACE AND SOCIETY

RACE AND CLASS IN RURAL BRAZIL

edited by
CHARLES WAGLEY
Columbia University

photographs by
Pierre VERGER

UNESCO

Published by the United Nations
Educational, Scientific and Cultural Organization
Place de Fontenoy, Paris-7e
1st edition December 1952
2nd edition December 1963
Printed by Meijer Offset, Wormerveer (Holland)

In 1950, at its fifth session, the General Conference of Unesco decided to undertake a series of studies on race relations in Brazil. The aims were to determine the economic, political, cultural and psychological factors which influence such relations.

The first book to be published as a result of the Unesco programme in Brazil was *Race and Class in Rural Brazil*. As was made clear in the original preface, the authors were given considerable liberty not only to present their material in the manner best suited to the societies described but also to draw their own conclusions concerning the race relations observed in those societies. Thus, while the opinions expressed are to be considered as those of the authors themselves and not necessarily as representing the views of Unesco, these first published results of the research programme set an example that was not only valuable in itself but also an auspicious beginning for the work that was to follow.

In subsequent years other volumes appeared: *O Negro in Rio de Janeiro* by L. A. Costa Pinto (*Brasiliana*, Vol. 276, Companhia Editora Nacional, São Paulo, 1953); *Les élites de couleur dans une ville brésilienne* by Thales de Azevedo (Unesco, Paris, 1953);[1] *Relações Raciais entre Preto e Brancos em São Paulo*, edited by Roger Bastide and Florestan Fernandes (Editora Anhembi Limitada, São Paulo, 1955); and *Religião e Relações Raciais* by Rene Ribeiro (Ministerio de Educação e Cultura, Rio de Janeiro, 1956). These studies cover a wide spectrum of the Brazilian social scene—small rural communities of the Amazon and the north-east; the old traditional cities of the north and the dynamic cities of the south. Together with the excellent recent study, stimulated by the Unesco programme, by Fernando Henrique Cardoso and Octavio Ianni in Florianopolis in Santa Catarina entitled *Côr e Mobilidade Social em Florianopolis* (*Brasiliana*, Vol. 307, Companhia Editora Nacional, São Paulo, 1960), they give us a full picture of the relations between people of different 'social races' (to use Charles Wagley's term) in contemporary Brazil.

In addition, during the years that followed the first edition of this work, further studies were to set the same communities that it had described against a larger background. The editor, Charles Wagley, published *Amazon Town: a Study of Man in the Tropics* (The Macmillan Company, New York, 1953); Marvin Harris wrote his book on Minas Velhas entitled *Town and Country in Brazil* (Columbia University Press, New York, 1956); and Harry W. Hutchinson has given us *Village and Plantation Life in Northeastern Brazil* (Uni-

1. Translation in Portuguese entitled *As elites de Côr*, *Brasiliana*, Vol. 282, Companhia Editora Nacional, São Paulo, 1955.

versity of Washington Press, Seattle, 1957) which treats Vila Reconcavo more thoroughly and from other points of view. We still lack a larger study of Monteserrat in the arid north-east of Brazil.

Yet, despite the time that has elapsed, the extension of research in this area and the changes that have taken place in a society as dynamic as that of present-day Brazil, the particular situation with which this work is concerned remains fundamentally the same. The traditional patterns of race relations described here are still to be observed throughout the country, although perhaps manifested in new ways in certain circumstances. The highly personalized relations between people of different social classes and different 'social races' in north Brazil continue to be maintained, while in the south life is more impersonal. But racial origin has not become a serious point of conflict in Brazilian society. Brazilians can still call their society a racial democracy. Thus the book preserves its original validity and much of what it says of particular parts of the country has been shown by more recent studies to be of wider application as well. Brazil remains as a lesson in racial democracy for the rest of the world.

This report is the outcome of an agreement entered into by the Fundação para o Desenvolvimento da Ciência na Bahia and the Division of Social Sciences of Unesco. It also represents the first results of a fairly extensive

PREFACE TO THE FIRST EDITION

research programme in the fields of sociology and social anthropology undertaken by the *Fundação* in co-operation with the Department of Anthropology of Columbia University. Three of the papers included in this report, namely those by Harry W. Hutchinson on the Bahian Recôncavo region, by Marvin Harris on the mountainous region of Central Brazil, and by Ben Zimmerman on the arid *sertão* region of north-eastern Bahia State, are based on field research performed in the State of Bahia during the course of this research programme. The scope of this State of Bahia–Columbia University research programme was much wider than the subject matter treated in this report, including also three intensive studies of Bahia communities which emphasized the process of social and cultural change now under way or in three different zones of the state.[1]

The field work in these Bahia communities began in July 1950 and ended in June 1951; it was carried out by the authors of the papers which follow with the help of various Brazilian assistants. The research programme was directed by Charles Wagley of Columbia University, Thales de Azevedo of the University of Bahia, and Luís A. Costa Pinto of the University of Brazil.

Late in 1950, Unesco—through Dr. Alfred Métraux who visited us in the field programme suggested that our field research be extended to include a more specific study of the general field of race relations, an aspect of Bahia rural life which would otherwise have been covered only as it related to our primary research interests. We were thus able to combine the research which had already begun in Bahia with the Unesco programme for the study of race relations in Brazil. This agreement with Unesco increased the scope of our research and, we hope, its significance.

The fourth paper of this report, namely that concerning a community in the Amazon Valley, written by the editor, is based upon field data collected in 1948 and during earlier visits to the Brazilian Amazon. The field investigation carried out in the Amazon Valley in 1948 was a part of the preliminary surveys carried out by Unesco for the International Institute of the Hylean Amazon, and preceded by two years the State of Bahia–Columbia University research and Unesco programmes for study of race relations in Brazil. Thus the

[1] The research plans and purposes of the State of Bahia–Columbia University research programme are described in *Uma Pesquisa sôbre a Vida Social no Estado da Bahia* (Publicações do Museu do Estado, No. 11, Bahia, Brazil, 1950) by Charles Wagley, Thales de Azevedo and Luís A. Costa Pinto.

data available on this aspect of life in the Amazon community are neither as full nor as precise for the other three communities, where specific attention was given to race relations during field research. A paper on race relations in an Amazon community was included in this report, however, because it provided us with a fourth 'case history' from another important natural and cultural region of rural Brazil. The community studied in the Amazon region, furthermore, occupies a position in that region roughly analogous to that of the communities studied in Bahia State, and thus offers comparable data on race relations in rural Brazil.

The papers follow a similar general plan of presentation, and attempt to focus upon approximately comparable aspects of race relations in each of the four communities. There was no attempt, however, to lay down a rigid outline to be followed by each writer; instead, the point of view was taken that each author should have full liberty to present his material in the manner best suited to the different societies being described. Likewise, each writer presents his own analysis and his own conclusions regarding the race relations in the community which he studied. It is the field scientist, who knows the community intimately and thoroughly after almost a year of residence and scientific research, who is best prepared to derive conclusions from his own data, each is therefore alone responsible for the paper which he has signed. The final statement, however, although written by the editor, represents the combined point of view of the group. Many of the points included in this last chapter have been discussed by the group in seminars at Columbia University, in meetings held in Salvador (Bahia) during the process of field work, and in New York during the preparation of this report for Unesco. In each case the descriptions included are part of more comprehensive book-length accounts of our field research which are now being prepared for publication.

All of us are indebted to numerous institutions and individuals. Proper acknowledgment and gratitude are expressed by each writer, but there are several institutions which sponsored and financed the research programme as a whole, and there are individuals to whom all of us are especially heavily indebted, whom we wish to thank as a group. It was the Government of the State of Bahia under the leadership of Governor Octavio Mangabeira—at first through the Secretaria de Educação e Saúde, and then through the newly-created Fundacão para o Desenvolvimento da Ciência na Bahia—which sponsored our research and provided us generously with funds for field study. The Viking Fund of New York and the Council for Research in the Social Sciences of Columbia University also made financial grants which made our research possible. It was Unesco which provided the funds for the specific research on race relations and for the preparation of these reports.

The strong and sincere support given our research programme by numerous State of Bahia officials and private citizens (too numerous to be mentioned by name) created an atmosphere and conditions for scientific research which would be difficult to equal in the world today. The magnificent hospitality, following the true Bahian tradition, which was extended to us, makes the memory of our sojourn in Brazil something always to be treasured. We are especially indebted to Dr. Anísio Teixeira who, as Secretário de Educação e Saúde of the State of Bahia, was the man who first saw the desirability and the utility of such research. Later, as Executive Secretary of the Fundação para o Desenvolvimento da Ciência na Bahia, he was an invaluable participant in our research, contributing his great knowledge of, and insight into, rural Brazilian life. To Professor Thales de Azevedo, who represented the State of Bahia in the research programme, all of us owe much not only for his constant scientific counsel, but also for his very great personal understanding and his warm friendship. We are indebted to Dr. Jaime Junqueira Ayres, President of the Fundação para o Desenvolvimento da Ciência na Bahia, for many energetic efforts in our behalf and for his moral and intellectual backing. We wish also to thank Dr. Alfred Métraux of Unesco for his good advice offered us in the field, for his stimulation which led to this report, and for his constant efforts on behalf of international social science.

CHARLES WAGLEY,
Columbia University,
December 1951.

CONTENTS

Brazil is renowned in the world for its racial democracy. Throughout its enormous area of a half continent race prejudice and discrimination are subdued as compared to the situation in many countries. In Brazil three racial stocks—the American Indian, the Negro and the European Caucasoid—have mingled and mixed to form a society in which racial tensions and conflicts are especially mild, despite the great racial variability of the population.

INTRODUCTION

by
CHARLES WAGLEY

The first period of Brazilian colonial history was marked by massacres and enslavement of the Indian population, and this phase was followed by a much longer one during which a large Negro population was held as slaves, and which lasted until as late as 1888. But, as several writers have stressed, the Portuguese colonizer of Brazil was as compared with many Europeans, singularly lacking in race prejudice, and in fact the Portuguese male colonist seemed to have felt a rather strong attraction to the darker Amerind and Negro women [1].[1] Whatever their feelings, it is an uncontestable fact that there was early and extensive miscegenation between the Portuguese and both the Indian and Negro. The *mameluco* the progeny of a Portuguese father and Indian mother, and the *mulato* generally the son of a European father and a Negro mother, soon became important elements in the Brazilian population, and race mixture continued for 400 years. In the modern population of Brazil there are people with the physical appearance of each of the parent racial stocks, and every conceivable degree of mixture between these three stocks is present.

Furthermore, in Brazil, a caste-like society with rigid barriers between the racial groups did not develop out of this slave background as it did in the United States and in the British West Indies. In Brazil, as the Negro and the mulatto gained their freedom, they were granted the rights of citizens and took part in public life. Numerous figures of partial or full Negroid descent became important in Brazilian cultural and political life [2], and there are such people today in high positions in Brazilian society, one in which racial tensions and conflicts do not constitute a costly drain on the individual and on national life. Today, it may be said that Brazil has no 'race problem' in the same sense that it exists in many other parts of the world; people of three racial stocks, and mixtures of all varieties of these stocks, live in what are essentially peaceful relations. All of them are Brazilians proud of their immense nation and sharing in its numerous problems and potentialities.

This does not mean, however, that all Brazilians have equal rights and advantages. Brazil indeed is a country of striking social

[1] The figures in brackets refer to the bibliography on page 15.

7

contrasts. There is a great difference between social conditions in modern industrial São Paulo or cosmopolitan Rio de Janeiro, and those in the backward frontier regions of the west and the north of Brazil. There is a wide social and economic gap between the wealthy who live in fine homes and modern apartments in Rio, and the miserably poor who inhabit the *favelas* (slums) only a few blocks away. Brazil has many social problems to overcome if it is to become a great nation with full social democracy. The standard of living of the majority of its people is well below that of most industrialized western nations. More than 50 per cent of all Brazilians are still illiterate. Transportation, industry, and agriculture are insufficiently developed to provide a sound economic basis for the country.

Nor will Brazilians who are aware of the social realities in their country deny that race prejudice is entirely lacking, or that a mild form of racial discrimination exists and is growing in certain areas. There are well-known stereotypes and attitudes, traditional in Brazil, which indicate dispraisal of the Negro and of the mulatto. There are also well-known barriers to the social ascension of 'people of colour' who are the descendants of slaves. Increasing discrimination in such centres as São Paulo and Rio de Janeiro caused the National Congress to pass a law making racial discrimination a criminal offence. Yet most Brazilians are proud of their tradition of racial equality and of the racial heterogeneity of their people. They feel that Brazil has a great advantage over most western nations in the essentially peaceful relations which exist between the people of various racial groups in their country. Industrial, technological and even educational backwardness may be overcome more easily than in areas of the world where racial cleavages divide the population. Brazilians have an important tradition to cherish in their patterns of inter-racial relations.

The world has much to learn from a study of race relations in Brazil. But objective field studies of race relations as they exist in modern Brazil are relatively few despite the great interest which students of race relations have in this 'Laboratory of Civilization', as Rudiger Bilden once called Brazil [3]. Such studies as Gilberto Freyre's *Casa Grande e Senzala*,[1] Sergio Barque de Hollanda's *Raízes do Brasil* [4], and others, have given us a panorama of the historical circumstances and of the unique factors which have produced contemporary Brazilian society, including its traditional patterns of race relations. Donald Pierson's excellent account of race relations in Bahia, *Negroes in Brazil* [5], although limited in its scope to the city of Salvador, comes to conclusions which are generally valid for a large part of the country. Yet Brazil is a country of accentuated regional differences both in natural environment and in cultural traditions; and, as mentioned above, there are sharp con-

[1] Translated as *The Masters and the Slaves*, New York, 1946.

8

trasts between Brazilian society and culture in the large metropolitan cities of the coast and in the small frontier communities of the interior. There are important differences in the 'Brazilian way of life' as it is lived by workers on large coffee, sugar or cocoa plantations and by those who cultivate their own land. Both rural farmers and plantation workers have a different way of life from that of the industrial wage earner. These and many other 'variables', so to speak, within the framework of Brazilian national society make for differences in the patterns of race relations.

The various research projects on the subject of race relations which have been stimulated by the Unesco project in Brazil should give us for the first time an objective knowledge of the situation as it exists under a variety of conditions throughout this vast and variegated country. The present volume is the result of one of these projects stimulated by Unesco. It is a study of race relations under rural conditions, but it is also a study, as the title indicates, of the relationships between social classes in the rural scene. It was soon apparent to all concerned with this report that race relations in the rural community could hardly be treated outside the context of the system of social class arrangements of the communities concerned. Or, to put it better, it was found that the most important and most crucial alignment in rural Brazilian society was that of social classes, and that racial type was generally but one criterion by which individuals were assigned to a social class. Race relations, then, must be seen as an aspect of relations between social classes, and as a part of a larger set of social patterns which determine the relations between individuals and groups within the rural Brazilian community. The form which this relationship between social class and race takes will be fully apparent in the chapters which follow.

To be more specific, however, the present volume deals with race and class relations in four small towns and in the surrounding rural zones in the vicinity of these towns. Since Brazil is predominantly a nation of rural dwellers, these communities are representative of an important segment of the whole country. Over 70 per cent of a total of more than 52 million Brazilians live in small towns of less than 5,000 people or in the countryside.[1] In the rural scene, many traditional aspects of Brazilian culture persist from the last century, less changed by the impact of modern industrialization, commerce and technology and by new values and concepts of the twentieth-century western world, than the cities along the coast. Thus, the picture of relations between social classes and racial groups which emerges from our studies of these rural communities is on the whole pre-industrial and pre-urban (in the sense of the twentieth-century urban complex). The patterns of class and race relations in these

[1] The 1950 census reported only 15,167,686 people living in *vilas* or *cidades* with more than 5,000 inhabitants. The total population reported was 52,645,479 (*Anuário Estatístico do Brasil, Ano XI,* 1950).

9

communities approximate to those which had taken form in Brazil in the last century out of the unique Brazilian past. Profound social changes have occurred in each of these communities in the last few decades, but each has retained much of an old way of life which is now old-fashioned or forgotten in the capitals of the country. In this sense, the patterns of relations between social classes and races which are described in this study might be considered more traditionally Brazilian than those now found in the large cities such as Belém, Salvador, Recife, São Paulo and Rio de Janeiro.

Modern Brazil is more homogeneous in terms of language and culture than most other areas of comparable size in the world. India, China and the U.S.S.R. each contain peoples of very different cultures who speak different languages. Even Bolivia and Peru, which are smaller in area than Brazil, contain large groups of people who speak aboriginal languages and whose culture differs from that of the nationals of the country. But throughout Brazil the people share one set of national patterns which were inherited mainly from Portugal, but which have been strongly flavoured by American Indian and African elements; throughout Brazil only Portuguese is spoken except by a small number of tribal Indians and some unassimilated European immigrants in the south. Thus, in all four of the communities studied, there is much that is common to all of Brazil, and especially to the innumerable small towns and rural areas scattered throughout the nation.

Yet this enormous country offers widely different environmental conditions. There is the low humid tropical forest of the Amazon, the arid semi-desert of the north-east with its dry streams and low thorny vegetation, the highly broken mountain range which forms a spine parallel to the coast for hundreds of miles, the semi-temperate south with its rolling pampa and pine forests, and so on. The European colonists soon found that these different natural environments offered different economic potentialities. Thus, the process of settlement and of exploitation took a different form in each of these regions. The basic economic pursuits, the composition of the population, and the traditions and customs which took form in each region worked, in addition to natural environment, to form regional versions of Brazilian national culture. Poor communications between one part of the country and another has led to the persistence of these regional differences.

Several regions of rural Brazil stand out clearly as distinctive natural and cultural units. Such regions as the Amazon Valley, the arid north-eastern *sertão*, the plantation region which stretches along the nort-eastern coast, the mountain and plateau region of Minas Gerais and the nearby areas of the States of Espírito Santo, Goiás and Bahia, and the semi-temperate region of the extreme south, seem to form well-marked environmental and cultural regions. Most

10

observers of rural Brazil would agree as to their general outlines. (See Frontispiece.) Other areas of the country, however, do not lend themselves so easily to regional classification. There are whole States, such as São Paulo, with their own traditions and with marked local varieties of Brazilian national culture. In a sense a State such as São Paulo might be considered a region by itself; but still, São Paulo dominates a larger area extending inland into Mato Grosso, Santa Catarina and Goiás. And there are more limited areas, such as the cocoa zone of southern Bahia, which exhibit the same local distinctiveness as one of these larger cultural regions. Few students of Brazil agree in detail upon the division of the country into cultural or natural regions—for each tends to divide the country according to the criteria emphasized by his own field of study—but most of them agree upon several great regions and upon the essential fact that Brazil contains several widely varying ones.[1]

Each of the communities dealt with in the chapters which follow is representative of a different region of rural Brazil. The community which is called Vila Recôncavo is situated near the coast, in the region where sugar cane was planted in the sixteenth century and which witnessed a great period of prosperity during the seventeenth and eighteenth centuries based upon the great demand for sugar throughout the world. Most of the African slaves imported into Brazil came to provide labour for these sugar plantations, and even today there is a large proportion of Negroes and mulattoes in the population. African cultural influences and the particular set of patterns, involving the large patriarchal family and the master-slave relations which took form on these plantations, were important factors in producing contemporary class and race relations in this region.

Minas Velhas, the second community to be considered, lies high in the mountain region where the mining of gold and diamonds brought Brazil's second important economic cycle of boom and bust. Agriculture and grazing have since become the primary economic activity, but mica, quartz, iron, manganese, semi-precious stones, diamonds, and even gold are still mined. The mining industry was an important influence in the formation of regional society. Although a considerable number of Negro slaves were brought into the region to work in the mines, the relationship between the European owner and his slaves did not take the intimate and stable form that it took

---

[1] In another place I have divided Brazil into six regions—namely the Amazon, the arid north-east, the north-east coast, the Industrial Middle States, the Extreme South, and the Far West. See 'Brazil' in *Most of the World*, edited by Ralph Linton, Columbia University Press, New York, 1949, p. 226 ff. The regions used in the present report differ somewhat from those which I proposed earlier, since we are concerned only with rural life. A region called the 'Industrial Middle States', as proposed earlier, does not seem pertinent for our present purposes; in terms of rural life, the mountain region of Minas Gerais and the nearby States seems to form a natural and cultural region. See also Preston James, *Latin America*, New York, 1942, pp. 386–560, and 'The Cultural Regions of Brazil' in *Brazil: Portrait of a Half Continent*, eds. T. Lynn Smith and Alexander Marchant, New York, 1951, pp. 86–103, for a different regional breakdown of Brazil.

in the plantations on the coast. The more pecuniary relationship between the mine owners and the slaves who mined their holdings seems to be reflected in the relations between the Negro and the white in the region today.

The third community discussed in this report is Monte Serrat. It is situated in the arid *sertão*, not far from the Canudos which was the scene of the religious uprising made so famous by Euclides da Cunha in his Brazilian classic *Os Sertões*. In addition to the famous religious fanatics such as Antonio Conselheiro of Canudos and Padre Cícero of Joazeiro in Ceará, the region is noted for its Robinhood-like bandit bands, which until about a generation ago attacked towns and ranches throughout the *sertão*. In contrast to the two regions mentioned above, the north-eastern *sertão* has always been a relatively poor area. It is traditionally a region of cowboys—the north-eastern *vaqueiros*—and grazing has always been the traditional economic pursuit but small-scale agriculture carried out in dry river beds and in less arid localities provides subsistence for most of the rural population. A long series of periodic droughts have regularly laid the region waste, causing hundreds of thousands of people to migrate to other parts of Brazil. The colonists were poor; they could not afford many Negro slaves; and the modern population was formed out of the Lusitanian colonists and their *mestiço* offspring. There was no period of immense wealth and prosperity in the *sertão*. As a result the modern class system and patterns of race relations differ from those in other regions.

Finally, an analysis of class and race relations in the small Amazon town of Itá is included in this report. Itá lies along the Amazon mainstream in that part of the great Valley known as 'Lower Amazonas'. The tropical climate, the lush vegetation and the elaborate river system formed by the Amazon and its tributaries made it a distinctive region already during the colonial period. From the beginning, the basic economic activity of the Valley has been the exploitation of the products of the tropical forest. During the late nineteenth century and the first decade of this century there was a relatively short boom based upon the export of wild rubber collected in the forest; it was a period comparable to the earlier economic cycles of the plantation and mining regions of Brazil. In the Amazon, however, it was the Indian who provided the labour force, and the aboriginal population has contributed more to the Amazon population and to its regional culture than in any other region of the country. Unlike the situation in the plantation region and the mountain region, where the Indian disappeared very early as an active element in the population, in the Amazon region the Indian and the *mestiço* are important elements on the modern social and racial scene.

These four communities may be considered as 'case studies', so to speak, of the regions of Brazil in which they are found. We cannot say that they are 'typical' of each region, for these widespread areas all contain a great variety of communities representing different adaptations to their natural environment and varied degrees of technological and social change. But, in each case, the communities described in this report have been strongly influenced by the historical trends which formed the regional society and culture—they were selected because they have long histories. Vila Recôncavo was founded in the second half of the sixteenth century; Minas Velhas in the early eighteenth century; Monte Serrat in the late eighteenth century; and Itá in the first half of the seventeenth century. Furthermore, all these communities are thought of in their respective regions as 'traditional' towns—that is, they are considered to retain old traditions and customs which in many localities have been superseded by new influence from the outside. While social change has obviously increased in all these places during the last 20 years or so, modern technology, new industries, increased transportation facilities, and other innovations have not as yet worked for social change to the degree that they have in other communities in the same region. Thus, the patterns of social relations described in this report may be considered as 'traditional', even old fashioned, by people of more 'progressive' communities of these regions and by city people.

With the exception of Itá in the Amazon Valley, the communities studied are all of approximately the same size. Vila Recôncavo, Minas Velhas and Monte Serrat are towns of approximately 1,500 people, while Itá has a population of but 600 people. Yet in each case the present studies include, in addition to the residents of these towns themselves, a fairly large rural population. It is the population of the town plus the rural inhabitants or those of satellite *vilas* (villages) who are found within the social, commercial and, sometimes, religious sphere of the town, that we mean when we speak of the 'community'. This 'community' is not coextensive with the *município*, the county-like administrative subdivision of the State. It generally includes only a portion of the *município*, although in all cases the towns we have studied are 'municipal seats' (i.e., *sedes de município*). In Brazil, such communities are seldom clear-cut spacial units within which people have a strong *esprit de corps*. Often people have a greater feeling of identity with their immediate neighbourhood or with their small *vila*, but, the larger towns are in some degree, a focus for trade, for political and administrative affairs, for religion and for recreation. Although there is a lack of formal patterns of social organization to set off these rural Brazilian communities from others in the *município* and in the region, they form spacial units comprising a small town and a rural zone united by a close network of interpersonal and intergroup relations. Such communities contain a local social system—the face-to-face social horizon of most residents.

13

It must be emphasized that the studies included in this report are social and cultural in nature. They do not deal with the classification of man by either genotypical or phenotypical physical characteristics, but rather with social classifications which are based upon real and imaginary physical differences. They deal with socially and culturally defined categories of people, and with the relations between individuals and groups. In all four rural societies studied, a series of criteria are used to rank individuals and groups in a prestige hierarchy. 'Social race' (i.e., the way in which the members of society classify each other by physical characteristics) is but one of a series of values which give individuals rank and determine their social relations. Throughout this report, when the term 'race' is used, the authors hold no brief for its validity as a physical or genetic classification. In one sense or another, the term is always used in this volume in a social and cultural sense. It is well known that colour or race data in population statistics reflect the social categories of the census takers, and it is interesting to reflect upon the variety of social definitions of 'race' which would inevitably be involved in any census of Brazil, especially in view of the information furnished in the chapters that follow. Even our own observations as to the probable 'racial' affiliation of an individual or group of people are by necessity 'naked eye' judgments certainly coloured by our own social and cultural experience. Throughout this report, then, we are interested in the social definitions of 'race' and of 'classes', and in their effects upon the life of the people of the communities studied, while exact physical classification is of little interest for our purposes.

Finally, it is our hope that this report will be of some use to Brazilians in viewing their own society with accuracy and objectivity, thus helping them to work toward a full realization of the tremendous potentialities of their great nation. In these studies, while rich traditions appear which must be preserved and strengthened at all costs, social barriers are likewise uncovered which prevent the full utilization of the human resources of these rural communities and which must be erased if Brazil is to become the great democracy it promises to be. Furthermore, it is hoped that these studies will be helpful, not only as a contribution to a larger programme for the study of race relations in Brazil, but in persuading people everywhere to view race relations in their proper context—namely, as an aspect of the social system of which they are a part. A study of the situation in Brazil makes this doubly clear. It almost might be said that 'race relations' do not exist in Brazilian society. This nation of people born of marriages between three racial stocks, and formed out of slaves and their masters, has developed a society in which in the relationships between people 'race' is subordinate to human and social values.

1. Freyre (1946), p. 11 ff.
2. See Pierson (1942), pp. 215–16.
3. See *The Nation*, Vol. 128, 16 January 1929, pp. 71–76.
4. Second edition, Rio de Janeiro, 1948.
5. Translated into Portuguese as *Brancos e Pretos na Bahia*, São Paulo, 1945.

RACE RELATIONS IN A RURAL COMMUNITY OF THE BAHIAN RECÔNCAVO[1]

by
HARRY W. HUTCHINSON

I. In the seventeenth and early eighteenth centuries, a narrow strip along the north-eastern coast of Brazil in what are now the States of Pernambuco, Alagoas, Sergipe and Bahia, was the most important region of economic, political and social life in the whole colony. The rainfall along this portion of the coast is dependable and the extremely fertile soil, which was originally covered with thick forests, was ideally suited for sugar cane. By the seventeenth century, this region produced a large part of the world's sugar supply. Sugar, which was then a luxury in Europe, brought fabulous profits, and the north-eastern coast of Brazil became an exceedingly prosperous colony. Large cities grew up along the coast; Salvador in Bahia and Recife in Pernambuco became the most important centres of colonial life, and Salvador was the capital of the colony from 1549 to 1763. Both were cities of great wealth based on the booming sugar industry. The numerous churches built in Salvador during the period of opulence, with their elaborate gold-leafed wood carving and polychrome tile work, are witnesses to the tremendous wealth of the era.

It was the plantation system, the basis of this lucrative sugar industry, which gave this region many of its characteristic traditions and formed patterns of race relations which have persisted in a modified form into the present. Gilberto Freyre in his monumental *Casa Grande e Senzala*, and other Brazilian writers [1],[2] have described life on these sugar plantations. African slaves provided the manpower. More than three million Negroes were imported from Africa during the seventeenth, eighteenth and nineteenth centuries, and a large proportion came to the sugar plantations of north-eastern Brazil. The Portuguese plantation owners became rich, and came to form a regional aristocracy with a luxurious and ostentatious way of life. The slaves and their masters, on these plantations, formed two distinct social groups, but it is distinctive of the region that their relations were intimate and warm; Freyre describes the intimacy between the *moleque* (Negro lad) and the master's son as playmates, between the master's wife and her domestic servants, between the Negro nurse and her white charges, and other close

[1]In addition to thanking those persons listed in the introduction to this series of articles for their aid and co-operation in making this study possible, I wish to thank the Henry L. and Grace Doherty Charitable Foundation Inc. and the Department of Anthropology of Columbia University, whose grants of funds contributed largely to the possibility of this study. Also, to acknowledge with thanks the aid of Carmelita Junqueira Ayres and Eliza Amelia Ferreira for their assistance in the collection of the data.
[2] The figures in brackets refer to the bibliography on page 46.

ties between Negroes and whites on these colonial plantations. All writers have mentioned the frequency of sexual relations between the white plantation owners and their female slaves. Slavery was not a humane institution in Brazil or elsewhere, but in Brazil relations between the slave and the master were of a more personal nature than in other regions where slavery existed in the New World.

By the middle of the last century, the West Indies and other regions of the world were competing with the Brazilian north-east for the world sugar market; and the abolition of slavery in 1888 caused difficulties of labour supply on these plantations. The sugar industry no longer provided the great wealth that it had in the past, and many of the old plantations were abandoned or sold to large commercial companies who installed modern equipment for large-scale sugar production. Plantation slaves became wage labourers, and the old traditional patterns of behaviour between the Negro slave and the white plantation-owning aristocrat began to disappear, to be replaced by an impersonal employee-employer relationship in keeping with the new way of life. Yet many patterns persist from the days of the old plantation system. Many of the descendants of the aristocratic plantation owners try to preserve the old traditions. They are proud of their family names, and large aristocratic families are still important in the economic and social life of the region. In many rural localities, there are still plantations where the relations between the workers and the owners are highly personalized, as they were in the past, and where customs and traditions formed during the period of opulence and slavery continue, if modified, by modern conditions. Throughout this part of Brazil, the relations between people of different racial groups have been influenced by the large proportion of Negroes in the population, by the importance of slavery in the relatively recent past, and by the particular form which the relations between the Negro slave and the European master took on the plantations.

II. The community with which the present article is concerned is called Vila Recôncavo; it is a real town situated in the zone known as the Recôncavo which surrounds Salvador, the capital of the State of Bahia, and which borders on the Bay of All Saints, extending inland from the shores of the bay some 30 miles on the northern side, and considerably less on the southern side. The Recôncavo was characteristic of the whole north-eastern plantation region. The Portuguese who settled in Salvador in 1549 recognized the value of these lands around the new city and the Bay of All Saints for sugar production. The third governor of Bahia, Mem de Sá (1557–74),

17

gave sugar growing a great impetus by organizing expeditions of soldiers which he led into the farthest reaches of the Bay of All Saints, killing, driving out or enslaving the hostile Indian inhabitants, so as to make the area safe for settlers to move out of the city into the surrounding area and plant sugar. Mem de Sá himself built one of the largest and most productive of the sugar plantations in the Recôncavo.[2] His lands comprised three and a half leagues along the coastline of the Bay, extending four leagues inland, and two islands.[3] This *sesmaria*—as the early land grants were called—of Mem de Sá was broken down into smaller pieces by his daughter who inherited it, and by the end of the sixteenth century, most of the *sesmarias* of the Recôncavo had similarly, been divided into plantations averaging approximately 600 to 1,000 acres. In the past 250 years, many of these have kept the same boundaries and names, but their ownership has changed hands many times and they have passed through many cycles of prosperity and depression.

The essential form of a plantation in the Recôncavo has changed little since the seventeenth and eighteenth centuries. In the past, the entire plantation was known as an *engenho*, taking its name from the sugar-mill building which was the heart of the plantation. There were two chief types of sugar mills, one operated by water power and the other driven by traction power supplied by oxen. Before the end of slavery, steam-driven machinery had also come into use. A typical *engenho* had four main items of wealth—its lands, its buildings, the livestock and the slaves. Most of the land was, of course, planted in sugar cane, but there were also wood forests to supply firewood, pastures for the livestock, and small areas devoted to the raising of food stuffs for the personnel of the *engenho*. The buildings of an *engenho* included the sugar mill, the *sobrado*, or home of the owner, and the slave quarters. The owner's house was frequently a very large and pretentious building with one and a half or two storeys. In the Recôncavo the landowners sought to build their houses *a meia encosta*, or against the side of a hill, giving the appearance of a two-storey house in front, but only one in the rear. Such homes were frequently constructed of stone, wood and mortar, with tile roofs. The slave quarters, which were known as *senzalas*, were generally long narrow buildings with sides of mud or *taipa* and and roofs of palm fronds. The livestock of a typical *engenho* consisted of oxen, burros, horses, sheep and cows. The oxen supplied the power to turn the grinding mills when there was no water power, and they pulled the large two-wheeled carts which were used to transport the cane from the fields to the mill. Horses and burros provided transportation for the plantation owner in supervising the work in the fields, and for him and his family for visits to nearby *engenhos* and to town. Cattle and sheep grazing on the portions of the land which were fallow supplied milk and meat to the plantation community.

18

1. Mulatto cowboy of the interior of Bahia

2. Cabocla of the interior of Bahia

The most valuable property of a colonial *engenho*, however, was the slaves. Comparatively few Portuguese came to the Recôncavo, and even those among them who had been labourers in Portugal did not come to Brazil to do manual work. African slaves had already been used on sugar plantations in the Madeira Islands, and a slave system was imported into Brazil along with sugar cane. Although it was expressly prohibited by the Portuguese Government,[4] the early settlers in Bahia enslaved the Indians who did not flee or who were not killed in the early fighting with the colonists. Governor Mem de Sá's Testament lists 95 Indian men slaves, 84 Indian women slaves and only 20 African slaves.[5] From the start, however, Indians were considered inferior to Africans as slaves; they seemed unable to adapt themselves to continuous labour in the fields and mills. Yet in many cases they were kept as fishermen, hunters and boatmen for the *engenho*, being in these activities superior to the newly-arrived Negroes. By 1700, the Negro slaves greatly outnumbered the Europeans in the region, and there were but few Indian slaves. Slave was almost synonymous with Negro.

An inventory of an *engenho* of about 650 acres, made in 1866 shortly before the end of slavery, gives a total value of 200 contos[1] for the *engenho*. The land, houses, slaves and livestock were valued at 125 contos; the value of the slaves alone was placed at 65 contos. The inventory divides the slaves into two categories: house slaves *(escravos de casa)* and work slaves *(escravos de lavoura)*. There were 18 house slaves and 103 work slaves. Among the house slaves were 1 barber-tailor-painter, 6 servants, 1 cook, 2 seamstresses and 1 apprentice seamstress, 2 sweet-makers, 2 laundresses, and 3 children without specific 'profession', as their occupation was called. Of the work slaves, 59 were listed as field workers (26 men and 33 women of all ages above the age of 12), 18 as small children, and 26 as specialists—including 4 ox-cart drivers, 5 sailors, 2 ironsmiths, 3 bricklayers, 1 field manager, 1 ship captain, 1 gardener, 1 barrel-maker, 1 specialist in the boiling of sugar, and 1 nurse. The prices of the slaves ran from 'without value' or as low as 20 milreis to as high as 1 conto 400 milreis, depending upon the age, physical condition and degree of skill of the slave.[2] The slaves were always listed in such inventories as foreign- or native-born and generally, if it were known, the place or tribe of origin was given. Many are listed simply as *Africano*. For those born in Brazil, the terms used are *Pardo*, *Cabra* or *Crioulo*; the diminutive form of these terms is used for all

[1] The *conto* is a unit of Brazilian currency, composed of 1,000 milreis. The milreis, or cruzeiro as it is also called today, is the standard unit of currency. In 1951 the milreis was officially valued at 5.27 cents in U.S. currency, making the conto worth $52.70. However, it must be kept in mind that in 1866 the value of the milreis was considerably higher.
[2] In 1835 this same *engenho* had 48 house slaves and 155 work slaves. The highest valued slave was 900 milreis.

those under 12 years of age.[1] Of the 121 slaves listed in the particular inventory mentioned above, 40 were African. Most of these came from West Africa. Of those whose African origin is indicated, *Nago* (Yoruba) is most often listed, and *Gege* (Ewe) is second.

On these sugar plantations of the Recôncavo in the colonial period, the overseer of all operations involved in the growth of sugar cane and production of sugar was the owner himself. Generally, only the oldest son was trained to take over his duties on the plantation; the younger sons were sent to Salvador, to Recife, or even to Europe to be educated as lawyers, physicians, engineers or Catholic priests. Daughters were married early and given their dowry, or they were sent to convents to become nuns or live as lay sisters. Marriages with first cousins were frequent. Every effort was made to keep the plantation undivided and in the family. The Recôncavo sugar plantation, until about the middle of the nineteenth century, was a remarkably stable community changing little in size and organization from generation to generation.

After the abolition of slavery, there was a partial exodus of ex-slaves from the plantations to nearby towns and to the capital of Bahia. The ex-slaves who moved to small towns became manual labourers or fishermen, or engaged in the profession they had learned on the plantations, such as barbering, bricklaying, etc. In other cases, ex-slaves rented small plots of land on neighbouring plantations to raise manioc, corn, tobacco and other crops which required little outlay of capital. Others became sugar planters on a, small scale; known as *rendeiros*, they rented a few acres from a plantation and cultivated sugar cane, sending the product to the nearby *engenhos* for milling. In other cases, the ex-slaves simply moved from one plantation to another, or they often remained as free men on the same plantation, still engaged in raising sugar cane, living under the same conditions as before, but legally free. Contrary to popular opinion, the *engenhos* of the Recôncavo did not all cease operations after abolition. Many of them kept on producing as before. In other cases the *engenho* or mill closed down while the plantation continued to plant sugar cane, sending it to a nearby *engenho* which was still functioning for milling. Some *engenhos*, however, did close down altogether and were abandoned, or went into the hands of receivers. At this time many plantations changed owners—wealthy people in the city were able to buy lands at a low cost and did so. But the failure of many of the *engenhos* in the Recôncavo was not a direct result of abolition, it was rather the continuation of an economic trend which had been going on for a long time. For many years previous to abolition, the plantations of the Recôncavo had suffered from lack of capital, poor administration, occasional crop failure, and

---

[1] In the inventories, *pardo* indicated light skin; *cabra*, dark skin; and *crioulo*, black. These same terms nowadays are used differently in the Recôncavo. See page 28 ff.

20

from the competition of other sugar-producing areas. Abolition was the factor which, in many cases, simply ended a struggle several decades old.

The overall production of sugar in the Recôncavo was already dropping noticeably at the time of abolition, and it continued to decrease afterwards. At the end of the last century, state-supported *usinas*, or large mechanical factories for milling sugar cane, were opened in an effort to stimulate sugar production. At the same time, various other *usinas* were opened by private capital. These central mills received and processed the sugar cane of many plantations. The *usina* had the advantage of freeing the planter from the worries of milling and marketing the sugar, allowing him to concentrate on higher production of sugar cane, while the mechanized *usina* was able to produce more sugar out of the cane, thus increasing production. This system of sugar production proved relatively lucrative, and the government *usinas* passed into private hands. The owners of *usinas* bought as many neighbouring plantations as possible, and in this way the *usineiros*, as they were called, became at the same time the mill owners and sugar-cane planters—employers of factory workers and of agricultural workers. The plantations which did not pass into the hands of an *usina* became *fornecedores*, supplying cane to one or another large sugar mill.

The *usina* system, however, in many respects did little to change the traditional plantation system. The plantations belonging to *usineiros* continue as separate units; each generally had an administrator, a man responsible to the *usineiro*, who is in charge of the plantation. As a rule the administrator, who is an employee of the *usina*, lives in the old *sobrado*, the former residence of the *senhor do engenho*, as the old plantation owners were known. The workers on the plantations and their families frequently still live in *senzala*-like houses, usually a long narrow building under one roof divided into separate apartments of two or three rooms. Despite many changes of technology, many examples of the old and the new exist side by side on these Recôncavo plantations. On the same plantation both mechanical tractor and ox traction may be used to pull plows. There are workers' houses side by side, one with electricity and a radio, and another using candles and kerosene lamps. Furthermore, the hierarchy of workers and specialists in sugar-cane raising persists little modified from the early nineteenth century. There are the field hands, the ox-cart drivers, the artisans and other specialists. The plantation is also approximately the same size as it was in the early nineteenth century (although several may be the property of one company nowadays) and it has about the same number of hired workers as it had slaves before.

But the *usina* system and other outside influences have made for many fundamental changes in the Recôncavo. In the very large

21

usinas, the mill hands and even the field hands are modern industrial workers. They are employees of a large industrial corporation and are protected at least theoretically by the labour laws of the nation. The highly personalized relationship between the plantation workers and the owner-administrator of his own plantation, which persisted from the slave era, has been replaced on the larger *usinas* by the impersonal employee-employer relationship of the modern industrial age. Today, modern plantations and small towns have electricity; there is modern housing for workmen; the State and even the sugar companies provide medical aid; there are primary schools both in the small towns and on many plantations; recreation facilities are found in the towns and provided by the *usinas*; and the sugar-cane experimental station situated in the area constantly urges fertilization of the land and modern techniques and methods of sugar-cane production. But the older and more traditional patterns exist side by side with the new, and each of them influences the relations among the racial groups of the zone.

III. Vila Recôncavo is a small town on the Bay of All Saints. The rural area around it, which lies within the social and economic orbit of the town and which is the unit under consideration, comprises some 80 square kilometres, or slightly less than half the entire area of the county of which the town of Vila Recôncavo is the county seat.[1]

It this area there are 14 plantations, three of which nowadays plant very little sugar cane. Parts of the town itself are built on the land of one of these plantations, and the rest of the town area is owned in small lots by private individuals or by the Church. Although Vila Recôncavo is the county seat, local government is the only important function which it fulfils for the surrounding area. It is not used as a shipping point, either for receiving supplies from the outside or for sending sugar to the outside. *Braços do mar*, or inlets of the bay, go to many of the plantations and are deep enough for the *saveiros* (shallow draft sailboats) used on the bay for transport. Many of the plantations have direct connexion with Salvador. Commerce in Vila Recôncavo is almost entirely limited to supplying the 1,462 inhabitants of the town and of some small islands and of one community near by which is not devoted to sugar production. It is not the major supply source even for these groups which live near enough to another and far larger commercial centre where they prefer to do their marketing. The *prefeito* or mayor of the county is rarely a resident of the town itself. Rather he is usually a planter of the surrounding area. He goes into town to do municipal business,

[1] Both the town and the county bear the name of Vila Recôncavo.

22

but spends most of his time on his plantation. The rest of the municipal officials are, for the most part, people who live in the town, although some of the town councillors are also planters living in the rural area.

The population of the area under study was 4,269 in 1940, an d is approximately the same now. Of this number, 1,462 are residen ts of the town. Of the total of 4, 269, only 17 adults (plus their 16 child ren) in the rural area are considered locally, and appear to be, pure Caucasoid. They are all plantation owners, and all of them also have residences in the city of Salvador as well as in the rural area of Vila Recôncavo. Living in the town are 14 persons (plus their ei ght children) who are also considered pure Caucasoid. Three of these are foreign-born priests, one is a doctor, one a dentist, one a state tax collector, one a federal tax collector, and two are young men who have married into town families. The others are the wives a nd sisters of the men in the group, although one of the wives is suspected of having Negro ancestors since she has to have her hair straightened while the others have theirs curled. There are five families and numerous other individuals in Vila Recôncavo who are called 'white', but whose ancestry is known to all as not being enti rely Caucasoid, and in the rural area there are even fewer. These p eople are known as *brancos da terra* (whites of the land), a term similar to the *brancos da Bahia* of which Pierson speaks.[6]

The two other elements which are present in the population of Vila Recôncavo and the surrounding rural area are the Negro and the Indian. As might be expected, the Negroid element in the population overwhelmingly predominates, and there are people who represent mixtures of Negro and Caucasoid ancestry in all possible proportions. The American Indian element appears in the people called locally the *caboclos*, generally from the arid north-eastern *sertão*, who are of mixed Indian and Caucasoid descent. These *caatingueiros* (literally, people from the low brush country of *caatinga*) and *sertanejos* (literally, people from the *sertão*) are not usually permanent residents of the Recôncavo. As a rule, *levas* or groups of these *caboclos* of *caatingueiros* come down into the Recôncavo at harvest time, from September to March, to work during the period when the *sertão* is dry and unproductive. Generally also, only men come, and they remain apart from the permanent plantation workers and at the end of the harvest head for home.

In Vila Recôncavo and its rural area, four social strata can be distinguished. First, there is a small upper class of aristocratic whites. This is almost an endogamous class, and intermarriage between first cousins is extremely frequent. The 17 white adults mentioned above are the members of the five families which locally compose this class. These families have been in the area for generations; two of them have been linked through first-cousin marriages for several generations. In the other families, marriages have been, with but one exception, with persons of equal class status, although frequently with aristocratic families from other parts of the Recôncavo or from Salvador. In the one exception, the husband was without wealth or much education, but he was known to be of pure white descent. All these families live *em família* (within the family), both in the rural area and in the capital, where they spend a part of the year. Traditional family and friendship ties persist among them. They are large families with numerous relatives in the city and in other communities of the Recôncavo, so that dinners, dances, card parties, anniversaries and other social events are generally within the extended family. Most of the males in this group have a profession, such as lawyer, engineer or doctor.

The second social stratum is a slightly larger group consisting of the bureaucrats of the town, plantation administrators, technicians and specialists of the sugar mill, merchants and professional people of the town, such as the doctor, dentist and schoolteachers. Persons in this group are for the most part descendants of local people, although the doctor, the dentist and several of the schoolteachers are from the outside. In this group, one finds the 14 'pure' whites mentioned as living in Vila Recôncavo itself, and five of them are members of a family of former planters. People in this stratum do not have residences in the capital. On the whole, this class is less well-educated than the class above it; it even includes people who have had no formal education whatsoever, and two individuals who cannot read or write. In this class are found most of the *brancos da terra*, many mulattoes and some Negroes, as well as the whites mentioned. This group might be termed the 'local upper class' to distinguish it from the small group of regional aristocrats mentioned above.

The third social stratum of Vila Recôncavo is by far the largest numerically. It consists of 'the people' *(o povo*, or simply *gente)*, fishermen, carpenters, bricklayers, mill hands, plantation workers, and all others who do physical labour. Fourthly, there is a smaller group of even less status in the community, the people without a regular and steady income—women generally without husbands, but with children, who earn their living carrying water to homes from the nearby spring or who work as washerwomen and domestic servants, and men who serve as porters and perform other very menial tasks and odd jobs. There are no people in these two lower class strata who are considered 'pure' white. A few are considered *brancos da terra* but the great majority of them are Negroes, mulattoes, and others of various degrees of race mixture.

The regional aristocrats reside only in the rural zone and maintain residences outside the community. The 'local upper class' is found in both the rural and the urban zones, since the technicians and administrators on the plantations are of this class, but mostly in the

24

town, which is the centre of the municipal bureaucracy. The upper stratum of the lower classes is also found in both zones, since it contains town-dwelling artisans and fishermen as well as plantation workers. But the stratum of lowest prestige, the people who live marginally in Vila Recôncavo, is limited to the town itself. There is no place for them on the plantations or *usina* of the rural area.

As has already been indicated, the major economic factor in the community area of Vila Recôncavo is sugar-cane growing and the manufacture of sugar. There are approximately 2,500 people dependent upon this activity.[1] Each plantation has its small community, with a store, houses, repair shop and the owner's house. Plantation workers live on the plantation, in houses belonging to it. They are paid according to the amount of work they do—that is, how much cane they cut per ton, or how many feet of planting they cultivate, etc. As a rule, there are only three salaried persons employed on a typical sugar plantation—the administrator, the *feitor* (foreman), and the *vaqueiro* (cowboy). The administrator is the most important person on the plantation, directing the work, making estimates for the forthcoming harvest, co-ordinating the cutting, transport and planting of cane, etc. It is the administrator who runs the plantation, who remains in the saddle all day overseeing the work, who checks on everything. The administrator is responsible only to the owner of the plantation, who generally acts through him. In nearly all cases the administrator is either a mulatto or a Negro. In two cases, Negro administrators are unable to read or write, but they are experts at their job and enjoy the full confidence of the owner and the respect of the workers. The *feitor* acts as the assistant of the administrator; he walks about carrying a measuring rod and a notebook, making note of the amount of work done by each man in the field. Frequently this is the middle step up the ladder from worker to administrator. As a rule, the *feitor* in Vila Recôncavo plantations is a mulatto, a dark *mestiço* (mixed) or a Negro as is the administrator. The *vaqueiro* is preferably a *caboclo* from the north. He looks after the oxen used for hauling the sugar cane—of which there may be as many as 90 to 100 head—and the milk cows, inspects fences, for the horses and mules, carries messages, and generally rides with the owner when he travels about from plantation to plantation. The three racial elements are thus represented among the high-prestige men of a typical plantation—the owner is Caucasoid, the administrator and the *feitor* are Negro-Caucasoid mixtures, and the cowboy from the *sertão* is generally of partly American-Indian descent.

Under this hierarchy comes the main body of workers and their families, which totals about 200 on the average plantation. Such

[1] Of the total population of 2,500 people living on the sugar plantations and at the *usina*, approximately 600 men are the actual cane field and *usina* workers. Obviously this permanent labour force is inadequate; it is supplemented by groups of *caatingueiros* at the harvest-planting season.

25

sugar workers move rarely, remaining for generations on the same plantation. Each family has its garden where a little maize, beans and manioc are grown. Pay day comes every two weeks, when as a rule the worker goes to the owner's house to receive his money. The pay is small, 15 to 25 dollars a fortnight, depending on how much the man has worked during the period. Men do not like to work more than five to six hours a day, from six a.m. to twelve noon, and seldom work more than five days a week. They work easily, without hurry. In the afternoon they work in their garden, if their wives have not already done so. On the plantation no one starves; everyone has his *patrão* (protector) in the person of the owner, and in case of an emergency, accident or sickness, he expects help from him. This personal element is very important on most plantations in the vicinity of Vila Recôncavo; as a rule, the owner knows all the workers by name, knows their families and their family troubles and problems. He is aware of their love affairs and up-to-date on the health of new-born children and their mothers. Nearly all cases of sickness, from common colds and rheumatism to more serious ailments, are brought directly to the attention of the *patrão* or his wife. The owner, returning from a prolonged stay in the city, receives visits from the workers or from their wives, during which all the personal gossip is exchanged. The workers inquire about the owner's family and more extended family, for they generally know them all. Engagements, weddings, births, deaths and illnesses are reported on both sides. Complaints or requests are also made to the owner. The relationship is highly personal, intimate, gentle and frank.

On one rather small *usina*, which will be called São Pedro, in the rural zone of Vila Recôncavo, the situation is somewhat different. São Pedro is not one of the large *usinas* of the Recôncavo, owned by a corporation; it is relatively small and owned by one of the most important families of the Vila Recôncavo community, members of the regional aristocracy whose family has held plantations there for many generations. Because the owners of the *usina* actually administrate it, and since they are in residence in the locality at least part of the year, they are able to maintain many of the traditional personal relations with their employees, many of whom have worked on the plantations belonging to their family and in the *usina* for most of their lives. But there is a total of 1,183 workers and their families at the *usina* and on the plantations belonging to São Pedro, and the very size of the enterprise and the number of workers make for a more impersonal and more strictly economic relationship between employer and employee. Workers become more a name on a payroll, and the employer a person with whom one seldom has direct contact. In the larger *usinas* of the Recôncavo this trend is even more marked especially where the employer is a large corporation with offices in Salvador.

26

The other important occupation is fishing and there is the new petroleum industry. In Vila Recôncavo, bureaucracy plays a large part in the economics of the urban upper-class. The municipal secretary, the statistics agent, the federal and state tax collectors and their clerks, the postmaster and various other 'white collar' positions belong to this small group. Often members of the municipal government divide their attention between commerce (owning small stores) and their government jobs. Despite its long history and rather easy communication with the large city of Salvador, Vila Recôncavo is still an isolated community. After landing in the town from the regular steamer coming from Salvador, one must proceed inland either by foot or by animal. The only motor vehicles in the community area (except for those of the petroleum industry) are a truck and a delivery-type pick-up truck owned by the São Pedro *usina*. One hears from all classes that the town is backward, abandoned and dead. It has had a glorious past: wealth, the large and beautiful *sobrados* of the barons who were *donos dos engenhos* (owners of the *engenhos*), two beautiful churches, a national guard post with almost 1,000 soldiers stationed in it, a record of bravery and leadership in the war for Independence in 1822, and a place worthy of a visit from the emperor, Don Pedro II. Today the *sobrados* are in ruins, or have disappeared completely, as today's *donos dos engenhos* remain on their plantations or in the city, forsaking the town. The military have gone, the splendours of the religious feast-days are no more. Vila Recôncavo is representative of the decadence which has overtaken the entire area. Today it is known only for its *xangó* and shrimps.

IV. In the United States an absolute 'line' is drawn between white and Negro. A person who is not white is a Negro, however small the percentage of Negro blood may be. In Vila Recôncavo, this 'line' is recognized rather than drawn. A distinction between Negro and white is always kept in mind when classifying an individual. Everyone knows who is 'pure' white and who is not. Classification by race is one of the most important aspects of local culture, and one of the most difficult aspects for the outsider to grasp. *Bahianos* of the Recôncavo feel that one may instantly recognize the difference between a 'pure' white and a mixed white-Indian, white-Negro or Negro-Indian, but they do not let it go at that. They classify or minutely describe each person; they classify according to skin colour, according to hair form and according to facial features, and their classifications or racial types are used in everyday conversation. Just as it would be said in the United States that someone is short and fat, the people of Vila Recôncavo will describe a person's colour and hair.

27

In the Recôncavo three race stocks are recognized: the white, the Negro and the Indian. A white is called a *branco*. The term *negro* is rarely used to denote a person of African descent. Rather such a person is called *homem de côr* (man of colour). *Negro* is used abstractly to denote the Negro race, but is almost never used to single out an individual. *Nego* (a softened variation of the word *negro*) may frequently be used as a term of endearment, even among whites, and sometimes as a nickname. When the *bahiano* of the Recôncavo speaks of *índio*, he usually thinks of the Indian of the interior of Mato Grosso or of the Amazon. When he wishes to indicate people of American Indian physical type in the Recôncavo, he generally says *caboclo*.

Yet even the whites are sub-classified, being divided into two categories, the *louro* (blond) and the *moreno* (brunet). There is still a third term for people with Caucasoid physical characteristics, but one which is used only by those who are considered 'pure' white— namely, *branco da terra*. A *branco da terra* is someone who is phenotypically white—that is, who has the physical characteristics of a Caucasoid: fair skin, fine features and 'good' (meaning *straight*) hair—but whose ancestry had Negro blood. He or she is generally *moreno*, and is frequently characterized by a slightly yellowish tinge to the skin. The *branco da terra* sometimes also shows traces of *caboclo* blood as well as of Negro and white blood. In Vila Recôncavo, the 'pure' white man may refer to such a person as a *branco da terra*, but ordinarily will call him or her a *branco*. To the majority of the population, the *branco da terra* is always called white, and no one would ever call anyone a *branco da terra* to his face. He is accorded the same treatment as a white by both whites and non-whites, and there is no constraint on anyone's part.

In classifying people, if skin colour is an important factor, hair form is equally important. If there is any question as to what to call a person, the hair is generally the deciding criterion. After skin and hair, facial features (prognathism, nose shape and thickness of lips) are considered. The many designations used in Vila Recôncavo for the people of Negroid or mixed ancestry can be broken down roughly into the following types in terms of these various criteria:

1. The *preto* or *preto retinto* (black) has black shiny skin, kinky, woolly hair, thick lips and a flat, broad nose. The *pretos* distinguish among themselves, and will rank themselves according to minute differences in 'quality' of skin colour, nose form, etc. The *preto* with the most *'qualidade'* is the farthest from the usual concept of a Negro, and yet still a black. He is a 'prettier' black.
2. The *cabra* (male) and *cabrocha* (female) are generally slightly lighter than the *preto*, with hair growing somewhat longer, but still kinky and unmanageable, facial features somewhat less Negroid, although often with fairly thick lips and flat nose.

The *cabra* and *cabrocha* generally lack the definite features and shine of the *preto*.

3. The *cabo verde* is slightly lighter than the *preto*, but still very dark. The *cabo verde*, however, has long straight hair, and his facial features are apt to be very fine, with thin lips and a narrow straight nose. He is almost a 'black white man'.

4. The *escuro*, or simply 'dark man', is darker than the usual run of *mestiços*, but the term is generally applied to a person who does not fit into one of the three types mentioned above. The *escuro* is almost a Negro with Caucasoid features. He generally has *qualidade*. *Escuro* is a very useful term for the outsider in the Recôncavo.

5. The *mulato* is a category always divided into two types, the *mulato escuro* and *mulato claro* (dark and light mulattoes). The *mulato* has hair which grows perhaps to shoulder length, but which has a decided curl and even kink. It can, however, be straightened. The *mulato's* facial features vary widely; thick lips with a narrow nose, or vice-versa. As a rule, the features are thicker than the *branco's* and thinner than the *preto's*. The *mulato* is generally distinguishable by a yellowish tinge to his skin colour, which is more accentuated than that of the *branco da terra*. His skin colour varies from very light to very dark. A *mulato claro*, with straightened hair, thin lips and a 'good' nose is very much like the *branco da terra*.

6. *Pardo* is a term not often used in speech. It is one of the official classifications used in the census and on identification papers. However, it is used occasionally to describe an individual who is closer to the white than a *mulato claro*. Occasionally *mestiço* children are described as *pardo*, before their features become distinctive enough to fit them definitely into one of the other groups. In one case, a little girl of three was called *parda* by her mother. The girl lives with her godfather, who is a *branco da terra*. He lists the girl as white, since her skin is very light and her hair is growing long and only slightly wavy. But her mother says she is a *parda*, because she knows that 'her hair may curl up any day, which would make her a *mulata clara*'.

7. The *sarará* is not difficult to distinguish. He has very light skin, and hair which is reddish or blondish but kinky or curled. His hair is described as *duro*, or hard. His facial features are extremely varied, even more so than the *mulato's*. There are *sararás* who would 'pass' for white in the United States, but more often the *sarará* has a curious appearance; skin which is neither dark nor light, frequently freckled, eyes with a greenish-blue cast and hair which bleaches easily in the sun. In Vila Recôncavo, the *sarasá* is usually found among fishermen and those living on the islands. It is difficult to see a person of this physical type without a good sun-tan and bleached hair.

8. The *moreno* has excellent skin, fine-textured and smooth. He is light-skinned but not white. He has dark hair, which is long and either wavy or curly. It is manageable and does not need straightening. His features are much more Caucasoid than Negroid. Here again we can distinguish between the dark and light *morenos*. Also we must distinguish between the *moreno mulato*, and the *moreno* of the white families—the *moreno branco*. *Moreno*, as used regarding the 'white', distinguishes the brunet from the blond of the same group.

Few people fit any of these 'racial' types 100 per cent. When someone comes very close to being a perfect *preto*—that is, has all the characteristics of the *preto*—people call him *bem preto* or *bem pretinho* (really black). The same is true of the *sarará*—*bem sarará*, or of the *moreno*, who will be called *bem moreninho* or *moreno fino*. It is just as difficult to find the perfect type for the other classifications, because there are so many variations. Often an individual is of one physical type, but has one or more characteristics of another type. For instance, one young man in Vila Recôncavo has the characteristics of an *escuro*, but since most people like him they prefer to think of him as *moreno*. He has fine skin and thin facial features, but tight kinky hair. People generally refer to him as *moreno*, adding '*mas êle tem cabelo ruim*' (but he has poor hair). One frequently hears 'he is *mulato*, but very light'. These verbal descriptions paint a vivid picture of the person in question. In Vila Recôncavo, it is not simply a matter of black and white, but of all the shades in between.

A term of classification not listed above, *caboclo*, presents something of a special case. As mentioned earlier, most people with Amerindian physical traits have come into the Recôncavo from the *sertão* during the dry spells in the North. Considering the length of time that people of the North have been periodically coming into the Recôncavo, comparatively few have remained. Nevertheless, the population of Vila Recôncavo has a considerable *caboclo* element —that is, of people with a reddish or bronze tinge to their skin colour, more prominent cheek bones than the African or white elements, and a tendency toward almond-shaped eyes. However, few people in Vila Recôncavo bearing these marks are called *caboclos*. They are classified instead in the local terms listed above, ignoring Indian traits. In Vila Recôncavo, there is a certain dispraisal of the *caboclo*. He is considered less civilized than the resident of the Recôncavo, though often known as a better worker, more ambitious, trustworthy, more frugal; also less genial than the easy-going person of the Recôncavo. In the rural area of Vila Recôncavo, each year many *caboclo* men come to the plantations to work during harvest time. For the most part they stay together, away from the *morador*, or resident worker of the plantation. The plantations construct a type of barracks to accommodate these men, who do their own cooking, care for their own clothes, and spend their evenings gathered around a fire, singing songs of the *sertão*, apart from the permanent workers.

There is a mutual desire to keep apart, for while the *morador* looks down on the *caboclo*, the *caboclo* feels very much the same about the local people. He feels that they are lazy, ignorant, and above all superstitious. The *caboclo vaqueiro* (north-eastern cowboy) of one plantation says that the workers of the plantation are always talking about black magic, that they are lazy and spendthrifts, and at the same time deride his frugality. He says he is not afraid of their black magic, since he knows there is nothing to it, but he distrusts those who speak of it. People in Vila Recôncavo will not admit they have *caboclo* or Indian ancestors. One young girl who is almost a perfect American Indian type says she is a *mulatinha*.[1] She vehemently denied there was any Indian blood in her family, but finally reluctantly admitted that a great-grandparent of hers had been partly Indian. This girl's niece would make a perfect double for the popular conception of Pocahontas, given a feather in her hair and a sarong, but she is considered a '*mulata*, almost *morena*'.

However, among the 'pure' whites there is a different feeling about the *caboclo*. White families say that they would feel proud to know that they have 'Indian blood', for it would show the length of time their family had been in Brazil. Frequently a white child is extremely 'Indian looking', that is, a *moreno* with jet-black, straight hair. The nickname of *tapuya* is often given to this type, which is generally admired by the whites. All plantation owners agree that, for work, no one can top the *caboclo*. The north-eastern worker of American Indian physical type will go into the fields at six in the morning and not return until six at night. He takes his lunch with him and eats it there. On the other hand, the *morador* will go to the fields at six and return at noon. However, as permanent resident workers, plantation owners prefer the Negroes of the Recôncavo. Little if any effort is made to 'fix' the *caboclo* on the plantations. When the harvest is finished, he takes his money and departs. Next year he may come again to the same plantation, or he may not. It seems to make little difference to either party.

There have been no serious tensions between the two groups. They work together during part of the year, but spend their free time separately. This does not mean that an occasional *caboclo* will not stay, take a wife from among the *moradores* and start a family.

The following percentages of racial types were taken from a sample of 162 heads of families, using the four major types: *preto*, 50 or 40 per cent; *mulato*, 59 or 49 per cent; *caboclo*, 3 or 2 per cent; *branco*, 11 or 9 per cent.

---

[1] Little *mulata*. Using the diminutive form seems to be a softer and more agreeable way of saying 'mulatto'.

V. Each physical type in Vila Recôncavo is thought to have a series of personality traits which are correlated with physical appearance. Furthermore, these stereotypes of expected behaviour reflect the attitude of people toward the various racial types present in the population. Two physical types, for example, the *cabra-cabrocha* and the *sarará*, are usually 'more to be pitied than blamed', as they are considered extremely ugly by most people. There is a feeling that they are unfortunate crosses between parents of physical characteristics which do not mix well. They are thought to lack the definite traits which characterize the other physical types and 'even a *preto de qualidade* is better than either of these—at least more handsome'. Furthermore, people of these physical types are thought to be difficult to deal with, irritable and easily angered. They are the physical types which are least preferred in Vila Recôncavo. All other types have some positive qualities. People arrange their preferences in terms of physical type in many ways, according to the qualities they wish to emphasize.

To the *preto* falls the more humble attributes of being a hard worker, of being humble and capable of loyalty and affection for his employer. He is also called lazy, a contradiction of hard worker. He is considered servile and cheerful. Also it is said that it is the *preto* who knows best how to please *(agradar bem)* the white. With a winning smile, pleasant little sayings and personal attentions, the *preto* knows how to make the *branco* feel important and puts him in the mood to grant favours. In other words, he is a good 'apple polisher', but even this he does with a certain dignity, aware of what he is doing, and aware of the fact that the *branco* also knows. The whites say that a *preto* is usually 'content' to remain *preto*, knowing that while he cannot change his colour, perhaps future generations of his family will have changed theirs. In Vila Recôncavo, people of all racial types, not only the whites, often say that one of the things they like best about the *preto* is that he does not try to be white. No one is more ridiculed than an *homem de côr* who, because of his economic situation and other circumstances, tries to be *gente*, or white.

On the other hand, a *preto* in good economic circumstances, who lives in dignity without pretension, is well thought-of by all. There is one outstanding example of this in Vila Recôncavo. A *preto*, who is the owner of one of the neighbouring sugar plantations and who is quite wealthy, lives quietly and without pretension. His sons go to school in the capital, one to Law School and the other to High School. His relations with the white plantation owners and *usineiros* are cordial and business-like. He would be acceptable at any social gathering he chose to attend, where he would conduct himself like a gentleman, without airs. For this he is admired by all, and pointed to as an example of how the *preto* can conduct himself.

32

On the other hand, the *mulato* and the *escuro* have the reputation of being social climbers. This is especially true of the *mulato* or *escuro* who has had education beyond the primary school, and who holds some government post or is a merchant or professional man. In Vila Recôncavo two mulattoes consider themselves as, without exception, the only cultured intellectuals in town. They lament the lack of companions to discuss poetry, literature, art and music. They are the first and loudest to say that the people of Vila Recôncavo are lazy, stupid, ignorant and superstitious. They are inclined to call all others *pretos*, and put as much distance between themselves and the *pretos* as possible. They say that they are much closer, racially speaking, to the white than the Negro.

At social reunions among the upper-class whites, a group of educated mulattoes is often present, and it is on such an occasion that all the pretensions characteristic of the mulatto are believed to appear, and that he shows himself a social climber who makes a fetish of correctness of manners, dress and speech. Pierson, writing about the city of Salvador, sums up the attitude of the Vila Recôncavo white toward the mulatto when he quotes: 'I resent their forwardness, their enviousness, their jealousy, their "lack of respect", their pretentiousness, their inconstancy and unreliability, their arrogance and (upon gaining some measure of improved social position) their overweaning pride, their boastfulness, cocksureness, "cheekiness" and general manner of showing off.'[7] Both the whites and the Negroes of Vila Recôncavo ridicule the mulatto, and when they use the term *mulato* with a certain inflection they convey the picture of a certain kind of personality. The mulatto, traditionally, has had the opportunity to advance socially, until today he is accorded much the same treatment given to the whites. Once on this level there seems to be competition between the two, and the insecurity of the mulatto seems to make for the above characteristics.

The other *mestiços* of the area resent this type of mulatto, whose actions as well as words indicate that he wants to be white as well as to be treated as white. Few servants are willing to work in the household of such a person. Many people who have the physical characteristics of a mulatto, but have not had the opportunity for education and other advancement, do not like to be called *mulato*. Instead they prefer *pardo*, which indicates the physical characteristics of the mulatto without the personality traits.

The stereotypes regarding the *moreno* are happier. A *moreno*, and more particularly *uma morena* (the female) is expected to be liked. The physical attraction towards such people is felt in all classes and colours. The *morena mulata* (mixed-blood *morena*) and the *morena branca* (white brunette) are frequently lumped together in the romantic national idealization of '*morena*'. The *morena* may adopt the ways of whatever group, and she will still be accepted. The *morena* is the darling of all the racial types, and she can do almost no wrong. There are also stereotypes regarding the white. He is someone who should not work, who should not get dirty or perspire because of work (in sport it is all right). The white is expected to be well educated, well dressed, wealthy, and to have power—both politically and as a landowner. He should also show a certain sense of responsibility toward those of the lower classes dependent upon him, protecting them against any violation of their rights, watching out for his *afilhados* (godchildren) of lower class, and distributing occasional favours. The white is addressed by the formal *o senhor*, while he in return addresses all others by the popular *você*. The white may also receive the very informal and affectionate form of address *yoyó* (for a man) or *yayá* (for a lady), which was traditionally used by slaves for their masters. Interestingly enough, it is usually the darkest of the *pretos* (even the most independent of them) who generally use this form of greeting. *Vossa Excelência* (Your Excellency) is also heard frequently when people of low status of an older generation address an 'aristocratic' white. Sometimes, whites are addressed simply as *meu branco* (my white). When the lower class refer to 'aristocratic white' or when whites talk of themselves, they may simply use the term *gente*, which means more than the simple dictionary definition of 'people': *gente* is synonymous with white, upper class, and wealth. The stereotypes regarding the white and, above all, the very terms by which he is addressed, are in keeping with his landowning aristocratic position.

This complicated classification of people by racial type, and these numerous stereotypes of the *homem de côr* by the white and vice-versa, are particularly striking in the Recôncavo. In addition to being simply a way of describing a person, like saying he is short or tall, thin or fat, they also imply what people desire in those of other physical types. The white wants good workers, cheerful people in whom he can have confidence. The *homem de côr* wants and needs a protector, a *patrão*, someone who will help him when he needs help, who will be godfather to his children, etc. But at times people will employ these terms in a derogatory manner. A white, displeased by something a *preto* has done or has not done, will frequently say *'que negro ruim'* (what a bad Negro!). But his *preta* cook may say the same thing of the *mulato claro* water-carrier who spills water on her kitchen floor. In the same way, a *preto* or *mestiço* who has been disappointed by a white may say *'que gente ruim'* (literally: what bad people!). Each of these two expressions has its counterpart of approval. The *'que negro bom'* (what a good Negro) has a wealth of meaning. Applied to whatever *homem de côr*, it expresses all that is warm and good that has developed during four centuries of close relationship between Negro and white. It is at once an apology for oppression and slavery, as well as an immediate thank-you. And for

34

the *homem de côr* to say '*êle É um senhor*' (he IS a real gentleman) or '*um branco bom*' (a good white) is to admit that the white and the Negro can live together in dignity.

There is a series of expressions used by all types to describe the person who is trying to appear white. Whoever tries to be what he is not is considered ridiculous by all. Both whites and Negroes gossip about the social climber and use the terms '*tem pinta*' (has a 'touch of the tarbrush'), '*tem sangue*' (has Negro blood), '*é da raça*' (is of the Negro race), or simply '*besta*' (show-off), '*cheio de arte*' (artful), '*cheio de manha*' (full of little tricks), or '*fala bonito*' (talks pretty).

There are also many phrases used by lower-class people to ridicule Negroes and *mestiços* who are showing off, or 'pushing'. Most of these start off with *Negro*:

Negro doesn't marry, he gets together.

Negro doesn't accompany a procession, he runs after it.

Negro doesn't sit down, he squats.

Negro in white clothes is a sign of rain.

Negro doesn't hear Mass, he spies on it.

Negro at a white man's party is the first to grab and the last to eat.

Negro's intelligence is the same size as his hair.

The concepts and fixed ideas which the people of Vila Recôncavo have of these racial types were also revealed in their responses to a pictorial questionnaire devised in the field.[1] A series of eight photographs of people unknown to those answering the questionnaire was shown, consisting of a male and a female of each of the four major racial types, the *caboclo*, the *preto*, the *mulato* and the *branco*. An attempt was made to use photographs giving no clue to the possible class position of the eight persons. However, the photographs which we were able to secure were not entirely satisfactory for our purposes in Vila Recôncavo. The picture of the caboclo male was of a man of middle age, but a type considered in the local conception as having a strong personality, while the *caboclo* woman was older and certainly not *simpática* (pleasant) in the local view. The two *pretos* were both unmistakably *pretos*, and both young. The *mulato* male and female differed one from the other, as the man was definitely a common *mulato* type, while the woman was almost a *morena mulata* rather than 'pure' *mulata*. She was young and considered much more *simpática* than any of the four women presented. The two whites were not distinguished in any way; and there was doubt in the minds of the people answering the questionnaire as to whether these two were 'pure' white or not.

The questionnaire was given to 85 people: 18 *brancos*—11 males,

---

[1] These questionnaires were given by a local assistant after the author's stay in Vila Recôncavo, but the results agree in general with the observations made during research in the community.

7 females; 41 *mulatos*—21 males, 20 females; 18 *pretos*—7 males, 11 females; 8 *caboclos*—6 males, 2 females.

Table I gives the racial types which were found respectively most physically attractive, most wealthy, best worker, most honest and most religious.

TABLE I.

Question	No. of people who selected in first place			
	Branco	Preto	Mulato	Caboclo
Most attractive man . . .	**39**	17	14	15
Most attractive woman . . .	26	3	**30**	26
Most wealthy man	27	11	9	**38**
Most wealthy woman . . .	**37**	8	17	23
Best worker, man	4	**38**	13	30
Best worker, woman . . .	7	22	23	**33**
Most honest man	11	22	8	**44**
Most honest woman . . .	15	13	22	**35**
Most religious man	21	15	13	**36**
Most religious woman . . .	17	11	17	**40**

Bold type indicates the group most frequently selected in first place.)

From Table I, it results that: (a) the ideal of the most attractive male is the white; (b) the preferred female type is the *mulata*, but the *cabocla*, it must be noted, is almost equally selected with the white; both the *mulata* and the *cabocla* (despite her apparent age) of the photos are of types which have the physical characteristics of the *morena* so preferred in Vila Recôncavo; (c) surprisingly, the *caboclo* male was selected as the wealthiest, in view of the stereotype that it is the white who is generally wealthiest, but I believe that this is due to the fact that people found the photo of the *caboclo* to have a rather 'distinguished' face, while the photo of the white was considered to be a young man with what might be considered a 'characterless' face; (d) the *preto* man was chosen as the best worker, which supports the stereotype discussed earlier, but the *cabocla* was chosen as the best woman worker (this may be explained by the local phrase used to describe her: 'Good for nothing else'); (e) the *caboclos*, both male and female, were chosen as most honest and most religious, which is in keeping with the stereotype of the *caboclo*, who is considered more serious and solemn than the native of the Recôncavo.

Table II, a breakdown of Table I by racial types, shows clearly the type selected in first place by the Negroes, the mulattoes, the whites and the *caboclos*, in answer to the same questionnaire. The most obvious inference derived from Table II is the extremely low position of the Negro woman in relation to the other women. She was chosen in first place in only one instance, namely as best worker, and only by the Negroes. In spite of the fact that in Table I the mulatto woman was considered the most attractive, she was chosen so only by the mulattoes. The other three racial types selected the *cabocla*

TABLE II.

| Question | Chosen in first place by | | | |
	Negroes	Mulattoes	Whites	Caboclos
Most attractive man. . . .	P	B	B	B
Most attractive woman . . .	C & B	M	B	B
Most wealthy man	P	C	C	C
Most wealthy woman . . .	B	B	B	B
Best worker, man	P	C	P	P
Best worker, woman . . .	P	C	M	C
Most honest man	C	C	C	C
Most honest woman . . .	C	C	C	C
Most religious man	C & M	C	C	C & B
Most religious woman . . .	C	C	B	C

(P—*preto*; B—*branco*; C—*caboclo*; M—*mulato*. Where two racial types are in first place, they received an equal number of 'votes'.)

and the white woman. In summing up the total number of 'votes', the mulatto woman won by a narrow margin (four votes). It is interesting to note that the Negroes chose the *preto* man as the most wealthy, putting the caboclo in second place, while the other three racial types put the *caboclo* first.

VI. There is a saying in the Recôncavo that where there was sugar, there were Negroes. This rule of thumb seems to hold remarkably well even today. On the islands in the bay where there never were *engenhos*, there are few *pretos*. In the town of Vila Recôncavo, and in a small settlement to the west of Vila Recôncavo where there never was an *engenho*, there are relatively few *pretos*, in comparison with the area of *engenhos* and plantations. The region as a whole can be shaded off in dark and light, to distinguish roughly the spatial arrangement according to colour. In the areas where there was and is sugar, there are many more *gente branqueada* (whitened people) than in the non-plantation areas.

These lightened areas seem to continue to lighten, while the darker areas retain their dark characteristics. In Vila Recôncavo, which is a *mestiço* community, there is much more opportunity for the lighter-skinned people for intermarriage with the mass of light-skinned people of the capital. Most of the townspeople have connexions of some sort in Salvador and travel back and forth a great deal. Some, mostly girls, take employment in the city as maids, and there either get married, or *'aparecem grávidas'* (show up pregnant), afterwards returning home to stay or for visits.

On the plantations the people have little opportunity for such mixing, owing to their isolation. Mixing occurs either on the same plantation or between neighbouring plantations, and since most of the plantation workers are dark, the offspring tends to remain dark. There is comparatively little marriage between people of the urban and rural zones.

The people of the town consider themselves far superior culturally to the *taberéu* or 'hick'[1] of the rural zone. Not only are they lighter in colour, but they are more 'citified', having more contact with the outside world, and this contact increases daily. Only in the town did the lower-class people express interest in the racial situation in the United States and particularly question segregation, a practice they could not understand. In the rural zone, the United States meant only some place other than Bahia. This is given as an example of the difference in degree of sophistication between the two parts of a comparatively small area. The sophistication of the townspeople tends to increase, as does their lightness of colour, while on the *fazendas* the colour has remained almost static, as has the degree of instruction.

Class is one of the most important factors in the everyday lives of the people of Vila Recôncavo. *Who's Who* is well known to all the residents of the community. Almost any resident will say that there are two classes, the rich and the poor. But definitions vary greatly as to what is rich, while practically all agree as to what is poor. Rich means, primarily, having money, a good house, more than one suit of clothing, a horse or mule, a servant to do the housework, and not having to do manual work. It also includes power of some description over other people. Poor is the reverse of all these things; working hard for someone else, a mud house with a dirt floor, one suit of clothes and one pair of shoes. For everyday ranking, this division into only two classes may serve.

A closer analysis shows that four distinct classes can be recognized, as stated earlier. There are many elements which go toward defining the classes—wealth, education and family. Race is also important. People say that wealth is the most important, education the second, and race the third in importance. Thus race is but one of a number of elements ranking people in a social scale, rather than a separating factor which divides them into distinct groups.

---

[1] Other terms used to convey the same meaning are *gente do mato* (people of the forest) and *gente da roça* (backwoodsmen).

In only one case can we absolutely equate a racial type with a class—the 'aristocratic white' of the rural area with upper class. The upper class of Vila Recôncavo is composed of a few families, descendants of the *senhores de engenho* (landowners), who have kept control of their lands, as well as having made a professional life in the capital as a lawyer, engineer or politician. They are upper-class not only in Vila Recôncavo, but also in the capital, Salvador, and their families are known in other great cities of Brazil. The horizon of these people is far wider than that of anyone else in Vila Recôncavo, and the scope of their activities is wider. Thus the gap between this upper class and any of the other classes is enormous. Nevertheless, the relations between it and the others are close, as this small class spends a large part of the year in the area and travels to it frequently during its stay in Salvador. There is little or no competition between this class and those under it, at least in the rural situation. In the city they are subject to all the stress and strain common to any 'high society' group.

In the rural situation this class remains, to a great extent socially apart from the other strata, but frequently a plantation owner gives a party for the *redondeza* (for the personnel of the nearby plantations). To such a gathering 200 or 300 people may come. The whites remain more as spectators than participants, but rules of courtesy and hospitality are rigorously observed, and guests are made to feel at home, without class differences. It is at such a gathering that the local *mulato* intellectuals and leaders will often attempt to show that they are closer to the whites than the other *mestiços*.

The chief class competition in Vila Recôncavo is between the second highest class and those below it. This second class, the local upper class, includes all the whites of the town, plus a large number of mulattoes and Negroes. As a rule it is this class which is the most conservative, the most anxious to retain its 'superiority', and which bears the brunt of pressures from below. This class will seize upon and magnify any element possible to belittle those who are, in any way, possible competition. It is in this group that the daughters are 'guarded', and have neither the freedom of the daughters of the plantation owners nor of the daughters of the fishermen. Ostentation plays a large part in their lives, and the men of this group rarely appear in the street without collar, tie and suit coat.

This group is also widely split by politics. Politics are one of its main methods for holding or advancing its social position, and they are taken seriously. Political scrapping has broken up the social activities of this group to a large extent, and there is more than one case of a family not speaking to another because of political differences. As a result their social activities are almost nil. They lead an unquestionably dull life, attempting to preserve a way of life belonging to the past, hard-put to maintain their economic status and remain gentlemen, with the result that they retreat more and more into a narrower scope of activity. This class is comparatively small, and while there is no upward movement to the class above it, there are many people hanging on its lower rung, coming up from below. Money will carry a person, whatever his racial type, into this group, although in the rural zone it is occupation and increase in money and authority which will elevate an individual, as in the case of the plantation administrator.

It is in the great body of the third class, the local middle class, that we find the most social ascension, or at least the most opportunity for ascension. Anyone in this class can better himself if he so desires, and once again it is wealth which is most important. Racial type enters here perhaps more strongly than in the second stratum; also the measure of desire to climb which the individual possesses. For among the majority of this class, there is what appears to be a lack of desire to climb. Perhaps this is allied with the past, with a strong heritage of slavery. At any rate, it is here that class and race are most generally confused.

Most people in this stratum who desire to ascend socially will say that it is better to be white, or at least light, than dark because it is the white who has the most money, the most education, and consequently most opportunities. Traditionally the light-skinned mulatto has been able to share to some extent in these things. Therefore, today, if an individual is lighter it will be easier for him to climb, simply because of his lightness. Upper-class people accept light-skinned people more readily—nevertheless, it is considered better to be a wealthy *preto* than a poor white.

For this class, after money, marriage is one of the surest methods to climb, and it is a fact that the light-skinned person marries *upward* more easily than the dark-skinned person. No one in any class likes a marriage in which the skin colours are too far apart. Any marriage of dark with light or white will be referred to as *mosca no leite*, or fly in the milk, and a certain repugnance is felt by all. One man, formerly a fisherman, but now a merchant of some means, is a *preto* married to a *branca da terra* who was poor but almost white. This marriage has not helped him much, as his wife did not bring him social position, but it has 'lightened' his children. His own status is increased through his financial transactions. But his children, who are lighter, are being educated in the city, and more readily acceptable because of their colour and their economic background. Their chances for a better marriage are greater than if they had the same background but were dark.

In another case, a white girl of the local upper class of the town is engaged to a *preto*, who is an engineer in Salvador, but whose family has roots in Vila Recôncavo. There was great resistance to

40

the engagement on the part of the girl's family, and all her friends felt that, although she had a good 'catch', that is, a successful man, he was too dark for her. This in spite of the fact that the girl's father is a *branco da terra*, and that her grandmother was dark-skinned.

One great bar between the upper class of 'aristocratic whites' and those below them is that of marriage. The white of the second class may sometimes be acceptable to the upper class, because he is white; but the chances are heavy against the marriage of an 'aristocratic white' with an *homem de côr*. Perhaps in the city situation a marriage between a white of this upper class and a *mestiço* of the same class would take place, but certainly not in a rural area.

Until the end of the last century many bastards were produced by the white plantation owners and their sons, with the slaves and ex-slaves. The Vila Recôncavo population is made up of a large segment of these individuals and their offspring, and in many cases they bear the name of the family of the white. So that today there exist in Vila Recôncavo people who are relatives to various degrees of the white upper class, and in some cases have the same family name. These people are not recognized socially by the whites. In many instances the mixed-blood has the family name, not because he was given it, but because he took it. Frequently a white family will keep track of the descendants on the illegitimate side of the family, and help them if necessary, but they would never introduce one of these individuals as a member of the family, even when that person has all the family physical characteristics.

In one case, the illegitimate daughter of a union between a slave and a white man recently found herself in a position to help the legitimate daughter of her father's cousin. This girl was born free to a slave, before abolition. The slave mother managed to educate the girl, who became a successful schoolteacher. Later on, when her father's cousin's legitimate daughter, widowed with three children, needed help to educate one of her own daughters, she found that aid from her *mestiço* cousin.

This type of race mixture is far less common today than it was some 70 years ago. However, young white men still frequently have their early sex experiences with *mestiço* and *preto* girls.

The fourth class, the lowest, is confined to the town and consists of people who have no steady employment and who have no *patrão*. They are people caught in the changing economic pattern of the area, from a highly personalized *patrão* economy to a more modern money economy. As yet there is no room for this group in the rural area. There are no 'pure' whites here—a few *brancos da terra*, and *mulatos* and *pretos*. Ascension from this class, which is very small, is easier for a woman, especially if she is light-skinned. For a man, only money will take him upward.

Traditionally the *preto* is linked with ignorance and superstition, and a most common example of his 'ignorance', cited by the upper strata of Vila Recôncavo society, is his belief in *candomblé*, the fetish cults of African origin so numerous in Salvador which have been described by various authors.[8] In the Caribbean, *candomblé* is known as voodoo and, as in Brazil, there is a mixture of Roman Catholic with African religious elements. In Vila Recôncavo there are highly complicated rituals of ceremony and healing, but owing to the pressures of modern life almost no one has the time necessary to spend in the full preparation for a *filha de santo* (servant of the god) or a *mãe de santo* (caretaker of the gods) and much of the old ritual is being forgotten and discarded, and newer and simpler innovations are in evidence. Another example given of the *preto's* 'superstition' in Vila Recôncavo is his participation in the cult of Janaina, the goddess of the water. This cult is really an offshoot of *candomblé*, Yemanja being the name of the African *orixa* or divinity, while Janaina is the name given to her by many of the cults in Brazil. It is Janaina 'who sends the fish to the fishermen', and they must thank her and give her gifts occasionally. Generally it is the *mãe de santo* who knows all the calls and prayers for Janaina and who presents the fishermen's gifts. Anyone who intends to climb the social ladder first disassociates himself from these rites, and then publicly condemns those who participate in them—although, in many cases, such an individual will continue secretly to give financial support to a local *mãe de santo* and to send gifts to Janaina. Often it is heard of a person: 'Oh yes, he is *gente* now, but last night he secretly sent his usual present to Janaina.' Individuals of all racial classifications belong to *candomblé*, although popular opinion has it that only the *pretos* engage in these activities. One can observe all racial types at a *candomblé festa* (ceremony), either as participants or as spectators. In one case in another area of the Recôncavo there is even a white *pae de santo* (male caretaker of the gods), a former lawyer!

Nevertheless, in Vila Recôncavo, there are examples of *pretos* and *mestiços* who have shown themselves capable of progress, with and without education. Two examples are the plantation administrators, cited earlier, who have risen to that honoured and relatively well-paid occupation in spite of the fact that they cannot read or write. On another plantation, the *feitor* has taught himself to read and write and is known as an excellent story-teller. Primary schools were recently opened in the rural zone of Vila Recôncavo, and night schools for the adults. The response has been great, people often walking long distances at night to attend class, in spite of the fact that one of the most disliked and feared things is going out at night.

In Vila Recôncavo, there has been a central primary school for many years, with an attendance of 354 of all racial types, children of the whites as well as those of the others, although no children of the

42

3. Caboclo of the interior of Bahia

4. A black cowboy of the Sertão

planters. People in the upper class of the town, when they can, send their children to the capital to continue their education, and there are several *mestiço* students from Vila Recôncavo studying law, medicine and engineering in Salvador. The intelligence of the mulatto is traditional, and it has been equally traditional that the darker-skinned person is unintelligent. Today these traditions are not as strong as before, but still it is felt that the mulatto has somewhat more aptitude than the Negro. The old idea of the Negro, meant for work and to be servile, still exists, now tempered with the knowledge that education can change the situation. There is only one club in Vila Recôncavo—a football club—and the players are all shades, from white to black, and so are the spectators. They all sit or stand together under the shade of the one big tree which gives shade to the playing field. The field is on the property of a white man who, while he has nothing to do with the team, allows them to play there, put up goal posts and markers. The bar and recreation centre are open to all so long as they wear shoes—a ruling made to keep out the muddy feet of children who came straight from the beach to have a 'coke'. All the racial types and classes get together here to play pool and gossip, this being the one and only point of public social activity in the town. At the movies, the admission price is extremely low, the same for everyone, and all four classes attend. Negroes and whites of all classes sit next to each other. At church there are no special pews, the faithful usually gathering in the front and the less faithful hanging about near the back. The choir and the acolytes are from all classes and colours. At parties, which are few, colour lines are disregarded, *brancos* and *morenos* dance with *mulatos* and *pretos* just as long as both partners can *pular* (jump).

The social situation is gradually changing, and the extremely personal element is being lost. It is strongest on the private plantation, where the owner spends the greater part of the year, but at the *usina* much of the personal element is weakened because of the numbers of workers. Even at the *usina*, there is visiting and gossiping between the owners' families and the workers. But at the *usina* not all the workers accept their subservient position as do those of the plantations. This is specially true of the higher echelon of specialists and technicians of the mill, who will frequently not go to a party given by the owner, even though invited. It seems to be a way of saying that the company of the white owners is neither needed nor wanted. They prefer to keep their relations on a strictly business basis. At the *usina*, when a worker is sick, he goes to the medical post where he is treated by a paid nurse, rather than to the owner's house. On pay day, the *usina* worker is paid at the mill by a paymaster, not in the living room of the owner's house. Nevertheless, in spite of the industrialized aspect of the mill, the number of workers is not too large to exclude all personal contact with the owners, who adminis-

43

trate and oversee most of the operations. This type of relationship has proved so satisfactory that up to date there have been no strikes, and no labour movements, or unions formed among the workmen of São Pedro. The length of time the technicians and other workmen of the *usina* have remained in their employ, refusing employment in other *usinas* and other occupations, has been a matter of pride to the owners of São Pedro.

It is on the plantations belonging to the *usina* that the white owner-*mestiço* worker personal relations are least close. The *usina* owners are able to make only occasional tours of inspection of the plantations, and therefore have little personal contact with the workers. However, the administrator has in many respects taken the place of the owner. He is the only man on the plantation with authority, and all complaints and requests for favours or help must be presented to him. In one case, an administrator has been on the same plantation for 26 years, and is well-known for the 'court' he holds. Once a year he gives an immense party for the entire community, and people from all four classes attend. He is wanted as godfather for the children of the workmen, and as *compadre* in their marriages. Nevertheless, the administrator is as much an employee of the *usina* as is the worker, and while the administrator can and does assume some of the attitudes and responsibilities of the owner, he cannot assume them all. However, it is a frequent saying among the white-owner class that the real owners are the administrators, for they are the group closest to the workers and to the land. A plantation with a poor administrator is not only a poor producer, but also means hardship for the *moradores*; a poor administrator will take no interest in them, and take little care of them.

In other areas of the Recôncavo, where the *usinas* are larger and more industrialized and where no owner resides either at the *usina* or on one of the plantations, but lives always in Salvador, there is only a paid representative of the corporation at the *usina*. In such large industrial units the personal element is almost entirely lacking both at the *usina* and on the company-owned plantations. There have been cases of labour difficulties, strikes, violence and the intrusion of political groups. In several instances, there are efforts today, on the owner's part to re-establish personal contact with mill and field workers, even on the largest of the corporation *usinas* and plantations.

VII. The relations between people of different physical types in Vila Recôncavo and on the surrounding sugar plantations have grown out of the plantation-slave system which flourished in the region about a century ago. Many patterns and attitudes formed in that epoch persist even today in the town and on the privately-owned plantations in the vicinity. There is the aristocratic group of whites descendants of the *senhores de engenho*—who form almost a caste, marrying among themselves and living out their own social life apart from the Negro and racially mixed population of the community. Just as the slave owners in the past, however, they depend upon the Negro and *mestiço* for labour; the Negro is pictured as the faithful servant and attendant of the white aristocrat. Again, as in the past, the mulatto who was the offspring of the European master and a slave mother is pictured as a social upstart and an intelligent trouble-maker. Yet it is the man of mixed ancestry who holds the intermediate economic and social positions; he is the minor bureaucrat, the technician in the *usina*, and the administrator and *feitor* on the plantations. The essential hierarchy has changed little since colonial times; and the relationship between these aristocratic whites and their Negro and mixed workmen is still a highly personal one lacking in social tensions, since each knows his proper position and each knows his rights, duties and obligations toward the other.

There is no race problem in Vila Recôncavo, nor does prejudice or discrimination work out as it does in other parts of the Western world. A Negro cannot become a member of the aristocracy, but a well-educated and economically successful Negro can have easy social relations with this stratum. Negro ancestry is without doubt a grave disadvantage in economic and social mobility, but there are no political and economic positions closed to a man of Negro or mixed descent. As yet, however, only a few Negroes have moved into high political or economic positions. There is only one plantation owner who is a Negro, and Negroes and *mestiços* hold only minor bureaucratic and political positions in the community. The *prefeito* or mayor has nearly always been drawn from the aristocratic white group, and has never been challenged from the Negro and mixed population. Yet in the town and among the mill workers, 'people of colour' are beginning to show independence, and unwillingness always to occupy a subservient and lowly position. The administrators like to ride better horses than the aristocrats, to have fancier saddles, to dress better, and to be more ostentatious than their employers. Many townspeople know the big city, and the essential class and racial democracy which exists there. There is competition to join the local upper class, and derogatory racial criteria are used to deride competitors who would like to rise out of the lower class groups into this growing upper class. African culture traits such as *candomblé* and the cult of Janaina are associated with low status, and people who would rise in the local social hierarchy are anxious to disassociate themselves from these groups.

As modern attitudes and ideology penetrate Vila Recôncavo, there are more and more problems of class relationships; the population is becoming extremely class-conscious, and there is an increasing desire to rise in the social hierarchy. In the rural districts physical type is less important than in the town, since there is less chance for one to rise socially, the positions of prestige being highly limited. But in the town and at the *usina*, the opportunities are greater, and therefore more emphasis is put upon racial type; although, even in the town, racial type is not the most important criterion for ascending the social scale, the most important being the possession of wealth and education. However, in the town, people who have wealth and education also show a tendency to 'lighten', generation after generation, as well as to ascend socially. There is no such thing as 'passing' in Vila Recôncavo, and there is no need for it, for many individuals who clearly show traces of Negro ancestry are called white and treated as white, with no constraint or embarrassment. Also there are no social activities closed to the *homem de côr*, provided he has the money and the education to take advantage of them. Physical attraction is also extremely important in the social acceptance of rejection of people, as is shown in the complicated fashion of classifying and stereotyping individuals, and the idealization of the *morena*.

In other areas of the Recôncavo, the personal element has been lost to a great extent, and has been replaced with a rigid class system, based upon wealth, personal initiative, education, racial type and 'luck'. For the most part, the tradition of the *patrão* is disappearing and people are more dependent upon their own resources in a more strictly monetary economy. Vila Recôncavo still however remains sufficiently isolated to preserve much of the tradition of the past, of easy-going personal relations between people of all classes and racial types.

BIBLIOGRAPHY

1. For example, Diegues Júnior (1949).
2. Wanderley de Araújo Pinho (1941), p. 28.
3. Ibid., p. 29.
4. Oliveira Martins (3rd edition), p. 30.
5. Araújo Pinho, op. cit., p. 49.
6. Pierson (1942), p. 139.
7. Ibid., p. 230.
8. Rodrigues (1935), Chapter 7. Pierson (1942), Chapter 10. Landis (1947). Carneiro (1948).

I. During the most prosperous phase of sugar production, the Portuguese in Brazil had never ceased to believe that greater wealth lay hidden somewhere in the midst of their unknown continent. At the beginning of the eighteenth century, the persistent dreams and rumours about fabulous treasures which would rival the riches of Peru and Mexico were suddenly fulfilled, at least partially. Gold was discovered all along the rugged spine-like escarpments which rise beyond the narrow coastal plain. These discoveries were centred in the area of Minas Gerais, but gold was soon found also toward the north in Bahia and the west in Goiás and Mato Grosso. In addition, a quarter of a century later, the pretty stones which kept turning up in the auriferous gravels were identified as diamonds, and the fury of prospecting redoubled in intensity. So great was the yield of precious stones that in one year the price of diamonds in Amsterdam fell by one-third, forcing the Portuguese crown to initiate stringent controls over the industry.[1][2] It is estimated that 44 per cent of all the gold produced in the world during the eighteenth century was produced in Brazil.[2]

RACE RELATIONS IN MINAS VELHAS, A COMMUNITY IN THE MOUNTAIN REGION OF CENTRAL BRAZIL[1]

by

MARVIN HARRIS

Streams of adventurers, reinforced by a fresh spurt of European immigrants, poured into the inhospitable backlands. The rush was similar to the Californian rush more than a century later. With the price of sugar falling on the world market because of new areas of production, many of the plantations on the coast were abandoned. Some plantation owners brought their slaves with them to work in the gold fields; others sold their slaves to the more prosperous mine owners. Minerals replaced sugar as the chief wealth of Brazil, and Minas Gerais became the busiest and most densely populated province. Hundreds of new settlements were founded, some of which, like Ouro Preto and Diamantina, rapidly became among the largest and most prosperous cities in Colonial South America. No small share of the wealth went directly to Portugal, where the court of Don João V came to rival that of France.

Few of the new cities could grow enough near by to feed themselves; the hills which surrounded them were mostly unfertile. In addition, mining consumed all the available labour. Food had to

[1] The writer is deeply aware of his indebtedness to the directors and staff of the Fundação para o Desenvolvimento da Ciência na Bahia who are cited individually in the preface to this volume. An Area Training Fellowship of the Social Science Research Council made the field work possible. Most of the material used in this article was developed in co-operation with Srta. Maria Guerra, Srta. Josildete Gomes, and Sr. Nilo García who were my able co-workers in the field.
[2] The figures in brackets refer to the bilbiography on page 81.

be brought in from distant areas. Cattle raised in the north-east fetched fabulous prices in the slaughterhouses of Ouro Preto. Roads were built connecting the food-producing areas with the mining areas and the mining areas with the coast. The growth of the city of Rio de Janeiro dates from the time it began to serve as the chief port for the exportation of mineral wealth, just as in the next century Santos developed owing to its proximity to the coffee-growing areas.

The period of intensive mining lasted about a century. By 1820 the richest fields were exhausted. The economy of the region gradually adjusted to the altered circumstances; farming was intensified wherever possible, and handicrafts and cattle-raising slowly gained in importance. The centre of population shifted from the barren hills and wind-swept plateaux to the more fertile plains and river valleys below the high escarpments. The population of Ouro Preto, which at its zenith was between 60,000 and 100,000,[3] dwindled to one-tenth its former size. None of the old mining towns were ever completely abandoned, however, despite their general impoverishment. This is true even of those towns situated in zones of almost totally unworkable soils. In many instances they continued to be bureaucratic centres long after they had ceased to have real economic functions in relation to the area which they administered.

11. One of these towns is Minas Velhas (Old Mines), an historic county seat of 1,500 people, situated in the south-central mountain region of the State of Bahia. Minas Velhas was renowned during colonial times for its social and economic opulence based on gold mining. Only traces of the gold and little of the opulence remain. It was one of those settlements which sprang up at the sites of the richest deposits, regardless of the availability of potential food-producing soils. Hence farming was, and still continues to be, a secondary feature of its economy. By the first quarter of the nineteenth century the surface ores had been exhausted, and the importance of gold mining steadily diminished. The town, in the meantime, had become an important administrative and tax-collection centre; a large predatory bureaucracy continued parasitically to scour an area many times greater than the economic sphere of influence of the town itself. Later, the *município* of Minas Velhas was divided and subdivided to form more than 30 different counties. The decline of gold mining and the rise of rival county seats, situated between the major escarpments in the alluvial plains where it was possible to develop agriculture, gradually forced a fundamental revision in the town's economy. Minas Velhas became the centre of a homecraft industry producing gold and silver jewellery, metal and leather harness parts, saddles, knives, whips and, more recently,

48

boots, shoes and sandals. This industry continues to be the main activity of the townspeople. But the heritage of the 'golden days' and the tradition of a bureaucratic *élite* has never disappeared.

Despite the fact that Minas Velhas has no telephones, water faucets, electric lights, movies, automobiles, tractors or refrigerators, the townspeople consider themselves 'urbanites'. Despite their isolation, owing to transportation and communication difficulties which have virtually made an island of the entire Brazilian interior, they are not and never have been complete strangers to the principles of city living. A literate concept of modernity and mode expresses itself in their desire to follow the latest dress styles gleaned from fashion magazines, in a rather pretentious social club, and in a town garden in the main *praça* (square) where ostentatious evening promenades take place. In no sense can the town of Minas Velhas itself be regarded as a folk community. Folk traits are not completely lacking, especially among the lower classes, but it is among the surrounding rural popultion that they are most commonly held.

The town is situated on top of an escarpment, 1,000 metres above sea level, in the midst of a zone of unworkable soil. A wide belt of uninhabited *gerais*—high plains covered with sparse grass, stunted trees, gullied slopes and ruined boulders—hems the town off from the rural settlements. The latter take the form of villages, clusters of farm-houses scattered about in the hills. They are found wherever an enclave of workable soil occurs in the barren mountain countryside. Owing to the widely intermittent nature of such soils, each of these villages constitutes a community apart both from the town and from the other village clusters. Yet these rural villages are satellites of the town in the sense that they are bound to it by political ties and by the weekly fair through which the townspeople receive their food supply. There are two main satellite villages within the social and economic orbit of Minas Velhas, namely Baixa de Gambá with a population of 250, and Serra de Ouro with 500 people.

III. The population of Minas consists mainly of two races—Negro and white—and the results of their intermixture. Occasional Amerindian characteristics may also be detected, but individuals of pure American Indian descent do not exist. In any rigid genetic classification few, if any, of the people of Minas Velhas would be either pure Negroid or Caucasoid; it is obvious that most of them are the result of Negro-Caucasoid mixtures. For the purpose of this paper, however, a refined classification is not necessary. As we shall see, the socially derived 'racial' classification, which alone has dynamic import, is related to physical characteristics in a flexible and subjective fashion. A simple four-fold classification, based on standard anthropological descriptions of racial phenotypes—namely, white or Caucasoid, Negro, mulatto and *caboclo* (mixture of Caucasoid and Indian)—will serve to give an adequate picture of the population. Based on a sample of 571 individuals (100 households), the distribution of these types is as follows: white, 42.5 per cent; Negro, 28.2 per cent; mulatto, 26.0 per cent, and caboclo, 3.3 per cent. This distribution may be considered as more or less representative of the town, but the population of the two village satellites considered in this study differs strikingly from the town's in its racial composition. In Serra de Ouro there are no Negroes, and in Baixa de Gambá there are no whites. Moreover, in both these rural groups less than 10 per cent of the population is mixed or mulatto.

The presence of Negro elements in the population of Minas Velhas is due principally to the use of slaves in the gold mines during the eighteenth century. The Negro village of Baixa de Gambá may well be the remnant of a *quilombo*, as communities of escaped slaves were called. Both popular tradition and historical treatises speak of a large *quilombo* near the Pico das Almas, a high peak in the midst of a rugged and still little-known wilderness not far from the present site of Baixa de Gambá. Whether this group (or groups) was composed of slaves from plantations or the coast, or whether they consisted mainly of local run-aways, is not known. The oldest resident of Baixa de Gambá, who claims to be ninety, insists that no one in his family nor in the community was ever a slave. He remembers that during his youth there were many runaway slaves who slept in the hills during the day and came down at night to steal food from the farms. The people of Baixa de Gambá had nothing to do with these renegades, however, and lived in fear of them. The failure to retain any memories of slavery suggests that his ancestors may perhaps have been members of a *quilombo*. Few persons in this rural group are aware of an African heritage, and the bondage of their ancestors is known to them only second-hand from persons who have learned something about the history of Negro slavery in school.[1]

In fact, throughout the area remnants of African patterns are few and incidental. From all points of view there can be no doubt that the social behaviour of the Negro and the mulatto is part and parcel of a regional culture in which all racial elements of the population participate. Not only are unmodified African traits rare but, when they do occur, they are not restricted to Negroes. The Negroes of Baixa de Gambá, like the whites of Serra de Ouro, have never even heard of the terms *macumba* or *candomblé*—the elaborate religious cults which are so deeply rooted in the Bahian Recôncavo and other

---

[1] The writer, the first American to visit Baixa de Gambá, was surprised by the extreme cordiality of the reception accorded him at the house of an influential *curandeiro* (folk doctor) who urged his family to 'treat our fellow countryman' with hospitality. Subsequent questioning revealed that the man had confused *africano* with *americano*, one term playing as vague a role in his world-view as the other.

areas of Brazil. They are all Catholics, sharing in common with other isolated rural communities the same underlying folk commentary on the official dogma and ritual, particularly with respect to *festas* and the magical interpretation of prayer. Elements of folk belief which are extraneous to the Catholic system, such as a belief in the enchanted nature of gold, the emphasis on the curative powers of herbs, the large body of dietary taboos and the various modes of witchcraft, are mainly of European origin and are shared by the people of Baixa de Gambá and Serra de Ouro. The crafts and agricultural techniques used in both villages are indistinguishable from the prevailing pattern of subsistence agriculture of the rest of the region. *Vatapá*, oil of *dendê* and other elements of African cuisine are not used. Perhaps the clearest example of African influence is the samba, which figures in religious festivals and at marriage celebrations as well as at almost any party. But the samba and other rhythmic forms are general Brazilian traits and persist independently of the presence or absence of Negroes. No evidence was found for any substantial difference in family structure or relations between the sexes between Baixa de Gambá and Serra de Ouro.[1] This is not to say that the presence of Negro elements in the population has gone on for several centuries without affecting certain important aspects of the culture, but merely that the resulting common culture is shared by whites and Negroes alike. In Minas Velhas and in the satellite villages there is no sub-culture which sets the Negroes apart from the other members of the community. It is against this background of a common culture that the relationship between racial groups must be considered.

IV. In Minas Velhas, the superiority of the white man over the Negro is considered to be a scientific fact as well as the inconvertible lesson of daily experience. Literacy only serves to reinforce the folk opinion with the usual pseudo scientific re-working into more grammatical and hence more authoritative forms. A school textbook used in Minas Velhas plainly states the case:

---

[1] It is true that the women of Baixa de Gambá seem to enjoy a less submerged role, participating in conversations on an equal basis with their husbands and being permitted a greater degree of activity outside the home. They carry produce to the fair, drink intoxicants in public view, smoke pipes, and confront male strangers with a minimum of coyness and timorousness. These features contrast emphatically with the role of women in Serra de Ouro—the white farming community—where women wrap a shawl around their faces and flee upon encountering male strangers, and where they seldom join in conversations conducted by males and never accompany their husbands to the fair. If anything, however, the behaviour of the women of Serra de Ouro is less typical of the region than those of Baixa de Gambá; the former are considered *exquisitas* (queer) by the townspeople, while the latter are merely considered rustic and ill-bred. Actually the racial composition of Baixa de Gambá is only a secondary factor in the modification of female roles. Parallel freedoms are enjoyed by the white women of the lower-class town dwellers. Many aspects of the way of life of the Negro segment of the population can similarly be traced to the fact that the main mass of dark-skinned individuals corresponds with the lower echelons of the social hierarchy.

Of all races the white race is the most intelligent, persevering, and the most enterprising... The Negro race is much more retarded than the others...[1]

None of the six urban teachers (who are all, incidentally, white females) could find ground to take exception with this view. They all contended that in their experience the intelligent Negro student was a great rarity. When asked to explain why this should be so, the invariable answer was: '*É uma característica da raça negra.*' (It is a characteristic of the Negro race). Only one of the teachers thought that some other factor might be involved, such as the amount of interest which a child's parents took in his schoolwork. But of this she was very uncertain, since the textbook said nothing about it.

Once when a small group of men was asked what Negroes were like, one of them, the mayor's son, shook his head and replied: 'Every one knows what a disgraceful creature the Negro is! But there's something I don't understand and want you to tell me. How did this curse ever come into the world in the first place when Adam and Eve were both white?'

'They must be sons of the devil' someone else answered immediately.

A Negro informant in Baixa de Gambá had a slightly milder version of the origin of the Negro: 'They say that Adam and Eve lived in a desert and had many children. One day Eve heard that Christ was coming to see them. She called them from their play in order to clean them up and make them presentable. But she only had one little pot of water. She washed as many as she could but there wasn't enough water for all of them. For the last two children she only had water enough to wash the soles of their feet and the palms of their hands.'

Another legend explains the origin of the Negro's inferiority in the following manner: 'In the beginning of the world God created two kinds of man—the white and the Negro. One day He decided to find out what their respective attributes were, so He threw them into the bottom of a well and commanded them to get out as they might. The white and the Negro tried to climb up the walls but without success. Finally the white, after thinking for a while, stood on top of the Negro's shoulders and pulled himself over the top. The Negro, left alone on the bottom, made no further effort nor cried out and was left to die. It was on this day that God decided to make the Negro an inferior being, and the slave of the white.'

In discussing the Negro as an abstract type, the white is inclined to deride and to slander. Many informants maintained that 'The Negro is more like a buzzard than a man', but such statements may vary greatly in emotional tone. They are rarely said with hatred.

[1] These two quotations are taken from *Geografia e História do Brasil*, a textbook by Gaspar de Freitas which is required reading for all schoolchildren in Minas Velhas.

The mood is generally lighthearted and tempered with earthy appreciation. There is no monotonous, heavy-handed under-current of bitterness or revulsion. This feature of the stereotypes held in regard to the Negro must be seen as a function of the Brazilian cultural ethos. The Brazilians are inclined to be light-hearted and gay; they laugh easily and their moods change quickly. In Minas Velhas, to the white and to a certain extent to the Negro himself, the Negro is primarily a curious, laughable anomaly. He is looked upon as a sport of nature, as a being with certain sub-standard and grotesque characteristics which make him amusing rather than disgusting. A white man will say: '*Negro desgraçado. Que bicho feio!*' (Miserable *negro*! What an ugly creature!)[1] and smile broadly as though he were speaking of some rare amusing freak.

The predisposition to laugh at the Negro rather than to hate him, and the prevailing mildness of the emotional tone accompanying the comparison between white and black, lead to occasional inconsistencies. The Negro is sometimes presented as a rather likeable creature despite his faults, as in many folk stories.

In such stories the Negro plays the role of a somewhat lovable trickster. He is as much of a scoundrel as the two white men but he is shown beating them at their own game. The triumph is possible because of an additional fault. He has an unsophisticated inability to control his hunger, and this the stories wryly transmute into a half virtue. If the Negro were shown in this light with any sort of consistency, emphasis on the derisive element would of course be unwarranted. As a matter of fact, however, this kindly view of the Negro's simplicity in no way contradicts the underlying devaluatory theme. Other stories which treat of the same characteristic of simplicity leave no room for doubt that the Negro's naïvety is meant to be associated with ignorance and not with cleverness. Many tales are told, for example, about Negroes who discover sacks of diamonds, mule-loads of gold, or buried treasures, and who instead of helping themselves to a fortune run to inform some white man, either their boss or (as slaves) their master. The white man, of course, takes all the treasure, becomes fabulously wealthy, and the Negro remains poverty-stricken. Negro informants emphasize in such tales both the lamentable child-like simplicity of some Negroes and the greed and dishonesty of some whites. The whites, on the other hand, simply ignore the implicit criticism of their honesty and conclude laughingly: '*O negro! Como é besta!*' (How stupid the negro is)!

The stereotypes regarding the Negro in Minas Velhas are flexible enough occasionally to permit him to reap advantages from his faults. It would be a mistake, however, to view the faults put to

[1] In Minas Velhas, as in most of Brazil, the polite expression for people of Negroid physical characteristics is *preto*. The term *negro* is a term of dispraisal, less strong than the American 'nigger' yet strong enough to give offence. Hence when translating from the Portuguese in this paper, the term *negro* will not be translated. *Preto* will be rendered as the English word 'Negro'.

best use as anything other than faults, or to view mitigated derision as admiration.

The same person may at one moment claim that the Negro is lazy and that 'he sleeps during the day', and at another time admit that 'the black race knows how to work harder than the white race'. The last, however, is not really a point in the Negro's favour, since the capacity to do the type of work implied, namely heavy physical labour, is scarcely something to be admired in Minas Velhas. The notions that the Negro is admirably suited for heavy physical exertion on the one hand, and that he is lazy on the other, seem to be in flat contradiction—the Negro is lazy, the Negro is a hard worker. But this contradiction does not signify any real ambivalence in the minds of the people of Minas Velhas. The *modus operandi* is dispraisal of the Negro on both counts.

There are other contradictions in the many stereotypes which are expressed in Minas Velhas regarding the Negro. But, like the one mentioned above, these contradictions are eventually resolved by showing dispraisal. One white informant, for example, who insisted that the white is better than the Negro in every conceivable way, quickly contradicted himself when it came to his opinion of intermarriage. 'The mixture worsened the quality of the white', he said 'but in this respect the Negro was shrewder than the white. He caught the white women and married with them. He made himself better in the exchange. He whitened himself. The white was more stupid. She dirtied her family while cleaning his.' Similarly, the picture of the Negro as naively honest, as expressed in the stories about his finding gold, is flatly denied in another in which he is shown to be cruelly dishonest:

Once there was a kingdom that was plagued by a dragon. The dragon wanted the princess. The king offered her as a reward to any man who killed the dragon. João, the hero, with the help of his dog kills the dragon. He cuts off its nails and the tip of its tongue. But a 'big black *negro*' who was looking for firewood finds the carcass and cuts off part of the tongue. The Negro hurries to court and claims the princess. The king gives a feast. In the middle of it João's dog enters and begins to eat out of the Negro's plate. The Negro tries to kil the dog. 'Who kills my dog must kill me first! João cries. Then he produces the tip of the dragon's tongue. The Negro is seized, tied to a mule and dragged through the forest until he is dead.

Thus in his attempt to devalue the Negro, the white inevitably trips himself up on some points. The Negro is honest and dishonest, stupid and cunning, lazy and a hard worker, naive and shrewd. But the fundamentally clear picture of the low value of everything that has anything to do with a Negro still remains.

The writer collected two long and unusually well-organized statements containing stereotypes regarding the Negro. They are both in

54

the form of rhymes with a verse for each letter of the alphabet. The first was taken from an illiterate farmer in Serra de Ouro who recited the elaborate poem from memory. Some excerpts follow:

In former times there wasn't so much disorder when there was an emperor and the *negros* had masters.

Everything about a *negro* is no good including his house which hasn't even got a ceiling. The only good thing he has are his teeth which God gave him so that he could tear rapadura[1] apart.

No one knows from where tihs nation came unless it was the work of a trouble-maker or a trick of the devil.

I don't know how the *negro* was born unless he was generated from the earth or was something that just happened.

They are very foul-smelling but there's no incense in the world that can make them smell better. No matter how little time I spend with them, I can't stand it.

The *negro* isn't human. God has nothing to do with him and the *negro* has nothing to do with the saints.

The *negro* has an ugly face. He spends the day sleeping and the night robbing farms. The tail of the snake doesn't rattle the night he's about.

A good girl would commit mortal sin if she went with a *negro*. No saint would excuse her if she yielded to a *negro* without being shot first.

The *negro* is always unsafe. What he doesn't steal he takes when no one's looking. To help a *negro* is a great mistake. When they see your foot they want your hand. I'm not going to help this animal because this animal is a thief.

If all the *negros* were to die, I would be happy. The *negro* in Brazil is like a plague on the wind.

Til[2] is the *negro's* letter. If it weren't for the *til* there wouldn't be the name of the devil (*cão*).

There are five accent marks that are used for our enlightment and to help penitence when praying before the cross. Rid us of the *negro* forever, Amen, Jesus.

The second 'A.B.C.' was written down by a group of men in Minas Velhas who had difficulty in remembering all the lines. Undoubtedly they improvised to a certain extent. For our purposes this adds rather than detracts from the value.

The *negro* came from Africa and spread out all over the world. He wasn't born of Abel but of Cain.

The *negro* is an ass and a brute. He's the cousin of the orangoutang, the monkey, and the chimpanzee. He isn't a person. All he's good for is to make black magic.

They want to be God here in Brazil, but they aren't good enough to wash the white man's feet.

[1] A hard brick of crude sugar.
[2] The sign for nasalization used in the diphtong ão.

It isn't perfume that makes a *negro* smell that way.

The mainstay of the *negro* is the sickle, the axe, and the hoe, and a whip in the small of his back.

The *negro* spends a lot of his time washing himself, but the more he washes, the dirtier he gets.

They say they are as good as us, but I don't agree. Unfortunately here in Brazil *negros* become doctors and lawyers.

If you've seen a buzzard, you've seen a *negro*.

When the negros read this 'A.B.C.', they're going to curse and call the whites 'porcelain of chamber pots' and 'troops of shameless yellow-skins'.

The *negro* hasn't got a face—he has a tin can.

He hasn't got eyes—they're lighthouses.

He hasn't got a mouth—it's a cave.

He hasn't got a nose—it's a tunnel.

He hasn't got ears—they're holes.

He hasn't got feet—they're slabs.

He hasn't got lips—they're rubber tyres.

His beard is the beard of a goat.

His whole face is satanic.

These defamatory sentiments are not confined to such rhymes. They have current and widespread circulation in spontaneous and un-organized forms. The 'A.B.C.'s' are merely a codification of general attitudes, and for the most part the similes and allusions they contain are common knowledge among persons who have never even heard of the rhymes.

Some specific features of the Negro stereotype are subject to the apparent ambivalences and contradictions to which we have already alluded; others, however, emerge as fixed and immutable principles which form the core of the white's attitude. These may be stated as follows:

1. The Negro race is sub-human and inferior to the white race.
2. The Negro does and ought to play a subservient role to the white.
3. The Negro's physical features, including physique, physiognomy, skin colour and body odour are utterly displeasing.

No amount of wishful thinking about the lack of 'race prejudice' in Brazil can alter these facts about Minas Velhas:

1. Racial stereotypes are well-developed.
2. The stereotypes are graded and arranged in ascending-descending order.
3. The Negro occupies the lowest level.
4. The white occupies the highest level.

V. The people of Minas Velhas recognize a great many physical types resulting from race mixture. These types are determined almost exclusively by hair form, hair texture, and hair colour; and by skin colour and skin texture. Physiognomy (wide lips, flaring nostrils, prognathism, etc.) is a tertiary consideration.

Among the most frequently distinguished types are: *moreno, chulo, mulato, creolo* and *cabo verde*. The *moreno* has wavy hair with the skin colouring of a heavily sun-burnt white. The *mulato* has crisp, curly hair, and is darker than the *moreno*. The *chulo* has crisp, rolled hair and his skin is the 'colour of burnt sugar or tobacco'. The *creolo* has fine wavy hair, is almost as dark as the *chulo*, but has smoother skin. The *cabo verde* has very straight hair but is the colour of the Negro.

All these different characteristics have different values attached to them — high if corresponding with the features of a white man and low if corresponding with the features of a Negro. Actually the correspondence is with something more general, namely the ideal of beauty, to which the white man generally approaches more closely than the others — this ideal demanding fine straight or wavy hair and smooth light skin. The important point is that the racially mixed individuals are seen as sharing a set of physical characteristics which can be used to judge proximity to two polar positions. The distance of each mulatto characteristic from white or black characteristics determines its value.

Beyond this, the writer was unable to discover any formalized stereotypes distinctly associated with the respective racially mixed types. In Minas Velhas there does not seem to be any 'A.B.C.' of the mulatto or *moreno*. What does occur, however, is that the set of physical characteristics by which the individual is judged to be more or less beautiful comes to mean to a large extent, more or less white or more or less negroid, not only from a physical point of view, but as regards behaviour as well. This may be stated as the following hypothesis: *The extremes of the racial ranking gradient are occupied by whites and Negroes, and the intermediate positions are occupied by racially mixed types.* If this hypothesis is correct, there should be in other words a continuous evaluatory gradient which is high for the whites, medium for the mixed types, and low for the Negroes.

Some progress has been made towards substantiating this point of view by means of data which can be handled statistically. The data are drawn from the results of a pictorial test devised by our field group for use in Brazil. The test as used in Minas Velhas consisted of three pairs of portrait photographs — a male and female Negro, a male and female mulatto, and a male and female white. The portraits were shown to 96 persons of varying colour, class, sex, and age. A sample was as follows:

	Class 'A'		Class 'B'		Class 'C'		All classes
	Male	Female	Male	Female	Male	Female	both sexes
White	5	5	7	7	4	4	32
Mulatto	—	—	10	10	6	6	32
Negro	—	—	10	10	6	6	32
TOTAL							96

The procedure was to lay down a set of portraits and ask the informants to select the subjects who showed most, less, and least respectively of a given attribute. Six attributes were inquired about: *wealth, beauty, intelligence, religiousness, honesty*, and *ability to work*. The response is shown in Table I for all sexes, classes, and colours, and for both female and male photographs.

TABLE I.

	Portraits		
	White	Mulatto	Negro
Most intelligent	**77**	62	53
Less intelligent.	68	**93**	31
Least intelligent	47	37	**108**
Most beautiful	**107**	75	10
Less beautiful	64	**98**	30
Least beautiful.	21	19	**152**
Most wealthy	**113**	46	33
Less wealthy	44	**96**	52
Least wealthy	35	50	**107**
Most religious	**82**	62	48
Less religious	64	**74**	54
Least religious	46	56	**90**
Most honest	**80**	70	42
Less honest	64	**74**	54
Least honest	46	56	**90**
Best worker	12	63	**117**
Worse worker	49	**96**	47
Worst worker	**131**	33	28

Note. Bold type indicates where the highest score falls for each respective type in relation to most, less, and least of each attribute.

The highest score for the mulatto consistently falls in the intermediate position. For the white it falls on the high extreme; and for the Negro on the low extreme, with the exception of the attribute 'ability to work', where the situation is reversed. Table II shows the totals of all six attributes combined as a progression in a three-valued ranking system. For reasons discussed on page 54, the highest score of 'ability to work' has been taken as the lowest ranking value.

Table II.

Ranking Order	White	Mulatto	Negro
1st	**590**	348	214
2nd	346	**537**	269
3rd	216	267	**669**

The results of this test illustrate another important aspect of the racial ranking system. The position assigned to each racial group in the scale of social value is similar, no matter which racial segment is consulted. Table III shows a breakdown of the three-valued ranking system as determined by each racial group in the sample.

Table III.

	Ranking order as seen by								
	White informants			Mulatto informants			Negro informants		
	White	Mulatto	Negro	White	Mulatto	Negro	White	Mulatto	Negro
1st . .	209	104	71	196	122	66	186	122	76
2nd . .	115	164	105	108	194	82	122	179	83
3rd . .	60	116	208	80	68	236	76	83	225

There is a slight tendency for each racial group to rate itself higher than the others, but the difference is never sufficient to alter the main outlines. The Negro rates himself highest a few more times than either the white or mulatto does, but this occurs too infrequently to change the over-all order.

The fact that the gradient was obtained from a sample consisting of all races and classes, and both sexes, ought not to be interpreted as evidence that there is no disagreement about the racial stereotypes, or that the Negro passively concurs with all the defamatory opinions of the white. We shall present ample evidence later that a *carte blanche* to slander is vigorously contested by the Negro. The failure of the Negroes' dissenting opinion to make itself evident in the test does not mean that the Negro feels he is irremissibly inferior to the whites, or that Negroes may not attain high social status. The results need to be explained in two ways.

First, the Negro concurs with the white in believing that he can achieve high rank never because he is a Negro but only in spite of it. All racial segments see race as one of the diagnostics by which an individual's value is measured. The Negro consistently tends to minimize and narrow down the negatively infectious scope of being Negro, and the white tends to exaggerate and broaden it. The white tends to strip the Negro of worth and dignity because he is a Negro, and the Negro tries to cling to his dignity and attain worth despite it. *But everybody believes it is better to be white.*

The second consideration is related to the extremely complex phenomenon of subjective and objective racial identification as it pertains to the test situation. This brings us to the threshold of the central descriptive problem of the relation between races. For the purpose of the racial apperception test, informants were assigned to the three broad racial categories we have been using, on the basis of their approximate similarity to the standard racial types. This procedure is faulty inasmuch as it does not take into account the frequent social and psychological transmutation which objective racial characteristics are likely to undergo. It is difficult to determine what portion of the 32 individuals classified by the observer as physically similar to the photographs of the Negro actually considered themselves to be similar to the extent of being able to make an identification. Many of those classified as Negro laughed heartily when they examined the Negroes' portraits: 'Is this a man or an animal?' one jested. 'How disgraceful! Look at the size of his lips!' exclaimed another. Since the society recognizes a continuum of racial forms from most white to most Negro with a large array of intermediate types, the tendency is to flee from the crushing stigmata of the lowest type by taking advantage of either slight physical deviation or by emphasizing social rank achieved on the basis of non-racial criteria.

The large number of intermediate types serves as a convenient mechanism for denying identification with the lowest. The Negro in Minas Velhas attempts to 'pass' not by posing as white but by posing as anything but a Negro—as a dark *moreno*, or *chulo*, or *caboclo*, etc. If these categories do not suffice he is liable to invent new ones. For example, a Negro storekeeper named Antonio who is well-educated by local standards, fairly prosperous and active politically, never refers to himself as *preto*, though physically he has every reason to do so. He prefers rather the original—and euphemistic—term *roxinho* (a little purple) and alludes to his son as 'that slightly purple fellow over there'. Each individual twists as well as he can away from complete identification with the lowest echelon of the social order. The Negro has the opportunity of saying first, 'My hair is not that kinky', or 'My lips are not that big', or 'My colour is not that black'; and second, 'I may look like that picture but I am not as poor, or as illiterate, as he probably is. Therefore, I am not like him'.

This denial of identification with the lowest rank is a common feature of most ranking systems. It is most frequently encountered in the difference between class structure as seen by the observer and as seen by the members of a given society. The bottom of any social order is a sort of Never-Never Land.

The real 'low-low' of the racial ranking system in Minas Velhas is not the Negro (*o preto*) but the invidious *o negro*. The Negroes of Minas Velhas will not tolerate being called *negros* because the term designates the impossible category of those who are not only racially but also socially black, in the most defamatory sense of that combination. The storekeeper quoted above felt it necessary to deny that he was a *preto*. This is a measure of his elevated social position. Negroes who are lower in the class structure do not feel it necessary to deny that they are *pretos*, but that they are *negros*. As one washerwoman put it: 'I am *preta*, but I am no *negra*, and I will curse any arrogant fellow who pretends so. A *negro* is somebody who practises black deeds, who has no morals, who has no manners. A *preto* is somebody who has dark skin and stiff hair but who isn't any worse than anybody else.'

Another important issue illustrated by the racial value gradient is that all positions are occupied to some extent by all racial types. The Negro scores at both extremes, as does the white and the mulatto. While there is definite vertical arrangement, there is no absolute horizontal discontinuity. Unlike what occurs in other parts of the world (for example U.S.A. and Union of South Africa), the Negro in Minas Velhas can be measured by the same yardstick as that which applies to the white. The Negro can be compared to the white even though on the average he may consistently emerge as inferior. The comparison proceeds not on an either-or basis—either white or Negro and, if Negro, non-comparable—but on a more-or-less basis: more or less like a Negro and more or less like a white.

This aspect of the gradient appears to contrast with the face value of the Negro stereotypes. In its extreme form such as displayed in the 'A.B.C.'s', the defamatory intentions of the white would seem to preclude the possibility of comparison by stating that the Negro is a creature apart, like a buzzard or a chimpanzee having nothing to do with God. But the fact that the Negro scores in the high extreme of the gradient does not alter the white's fundamental conception of the Negro as an inferior race. Actually there was not a single white informant who rated the portrait of the Negro higher than that of the white when it came to summing up the score for all the attributes combined: i.e., while the individual white occasionally rated the Negro higher than the white for a particular attribute, no individual white rated the Negro highest for the majority of them. The answers to the test must be looked upon as a form of response midway between the ideal and the actual behaviour patterns. The ideal pattern for the white clearly enjoins, wishes for, and tends towards a clear-cut separation of Negro and white destinies. In the actual behaviour pattern, as we shall see, this happens only to a limited extent. The gradient reflects both the wish or daydream of the white to be everywhere superior by showing himself to be consistently better in total than the Negro, and it also reflects the real situation where the white recognizes that the Negro is occasionally richer or more honest or more intelligent or more religious, etc., than the white is. The white's conceptualization regularly seeks to deny that the Negro can ever overcome being a Negro owing to his superiority in some additional non-racial characteristic. But even in the 'A.B.C.'s' we find references to Negroes as educated and wealthy men.

VI. The actual behaviour of the white towards the Negro differs from the white's ideal of what it ought to be.

A certain white man in Minas Velhas, named José Domingos, who in his youth had been a skilled metal artisan, has been going blind for the last 20 years. Ten years ago his eyesight became so bad that he had to abandon his profession. He now barely manages to keep alive by organizing *rifas* (lotteries) in which a can of kerosene or a ream of cloth is the prize. José begs the storekeepers to sell him the kerosene at wholesale price, then he goes from house to house asking people to buy a chance. In his entire demeanour—clothes, walk and talk—José displays to his superiors the abject deference of a beggar. Yet he was responsible for the following statement: 'A *preto* may be a doctor (that is, any professional) and have *posição* (status), but he always remains a *negro*. If you have a dispute with him over something you can always say 'You're a *negro*', and he won't have anything to answer back with.' Then he capped these sentiments by reciting a widely known quatrain:

> *Negro* even when a doctor
> Ought to be addressed as *tu*
> Because the worst race in the world
> Is the *negro*, the toad and the buzzard.

But how does José behave when he actually meets a Negro who has *posição*? When talking to Senhor Waldemar, the *vereador*, far from using the deprecatory *tu* reserved for addressing inferiors, José inevitably uses *o senhor*, one step higher than the normal *você*. A week after he had made the statement quoted above, José was heard in Antonio's ('slightly purple') store using *o senhor* and trying desperately to talk Antonio into selling him a can of kerosene at the wholesale price. Neither of these Negroes remotely resembles a *doutor*; there are none such in Minas Velhas at present. One day a full-fledged Negro *doutor* came to Minas Velhas. He was a State engineer sent to survey the possibilities for a hydro-electric installation at the request of the county. Everyone in town tried to sell him something, including José who tried to sell him a *rifa*. José told his tragic history and ended up by asking '*O Doutor, Vossa Excelência*' to please help him out.

Many similar examples of contradictions between ideal and actual behaviour could be cited. The Negro is supposed to have a smell

62

which nobody can stand for an instant, yet there was never an occasion in Minas Velhas when a white man left a room because there was a Negro in it. The Negro is supposed to be 'offered a foot' and the white man is indignant 'when he wants his hand', but no white man ever refused his hand to anybody because, and only because, he was a Negro. The stereotype speaks of the sub-human standards of the Negro as a father and husband and of the atrocious condition of his home. White girls are warned that self-respect and a Negro husband are incompatible, but the population itself is but one grand demonstration that this warning has never been completely heeded.

How then are we to consider the defamatory stereotypes? Is there any connexion between how the white tries to think about the Negro and how the white actually behaves toward him? Are the slanderous stereotypes a factor in race relations? The answer is an emphatic 'yes'.

To understand exactly how and to what extent this is true we must rid ourselves of the notion that the terms 'Negro' and 'white' denote clear-cut, readily identifiable physical groups for anybody but the anthropologist. It is true that in the ideal stereotype there is a group whose members are defined by physical criteria; in actual everyday life no group so constituted can be discerned. In every real situation the fact that an individual manifests a particular set of physical characteristics does not by itself determine his status. There is no status-role for the Negro as a Negro, nor for the white as a white, except in the ideal culture. In Minas Velhas the one and only inclusive system by which actual rank is established is that of class. All other ranking systems determine rank either incompletely or for only small numbers of individuals. Race is but one of several criteria which determine an individual's class and is thus but one of several criteria which will determine how the mass of other individuals will actually behave towards him.

In Minas Velhas the principal diagnostics of class, besides race, are wealth, education and occupation. Each of these, like race, can be expressed in terms of distinct, though interdependent, value gradients. All four gradients considered together have the power of fixing an individual's position in the social hierarchy. In addition, the value of any one of the four may be modified or offset by the values of the other three. Wealth, occupation and education have, in other words, to a certain extent the power of defining race. It is owing to this fact that there are no socially important groups in Minas Velhas which are determined by purely physical characteristics.

The idea that race can be changed by social invention is not as strange as it may seem at first glance. It is common enough that when there are a number of diagnostics by which the social value of an individual in a rank-conscious society is determined, not all of the diagnostics need be applied with equal conclusiveness to each individual.

In any society, an individual is most often thought to be higher or lower, better or worse, of more or less value, according to the extent to which he manifests a complex series of criteria. It is common experience that the emphasis placed upon any particular characteristic may vary according to the result of the total evaluation. The deficient quality, achieved or inherited, may not only be played down, sometimes to the extent of being completely discarded, but it may also benefit from a sort of transmutation. Thus, beauty for a woman is an important quality: the beautiful girl in our society begins with a prestige far higher than that of an ugly girl of comparable background. But an ugly girl who is rich, gifted in the arts, or otherwise outstanding in terms of some other evaluatory principle, may easily rank higher than the beautiful girl who is deficient in these respects. Moreover, while her ugliness does not thereby change as a physical fact, there will be a tendency to regard her faults euphemistically so that her features may be considered 'interesting' or 'striking' of 'full of character' rather than ugly. Most complex systems of rank are reciprocal in this sense—a high rating in one particular tends to obscure or raise the low rating in another. If the majority of indices each show high ranking status, the minority which do not are benefited by an infectious upward shift. If most indices are low, the few which are high suffer the opposite effect.

The failure to state this fundamental principle of rank easily leads to a distorted picture of the race situation in Brazil. An important characteristic of race relations in Minas Velhas, as well as in most of Brazil, is the occasional ability of individuals of low-ranking physical types to rise to otherwise high-ranking status. One of the members (*vereador*) of the Municipal Council (*Camara*) of the county of Minas Velhas is a Negro—Sr. Waldemar. This man owns considerable land and the town's only bar, and is sufficiently wealthy no longer to need to work. Waldemar is treated with universal respect by both whites and Negroes. One of his sons recently married a white girl; the wedding was attended by the town's *élite*, and congratulatory visits were paid to Waldemar's house by representatives of some of the town's best families. There is no doubt that Waldemar ranks higher in the class system than most whites (though for reasons to be discussed below he cannot be included in the upper class). From time to time other Negroes in the community have enjoyed comparable prestige. Such instances are few, however, and even if they were multiplied several times over the basic evaluation of a Negro as a Negro, and not as a rich Negro or an educated Negro, would still be the same. In the scale of physical types the position of the Negro is unquestionably the least desirable. High rank in other respects can only be achieved in spite of being, never because, one is black.

Much has been made of the expression which is heard in Minas

Velhas, as well as other parts of Brazil, that 'money whitens'. The unstated corollaries: 'Whiteness is worth money' and 'Blackness cheapens' also need to be emphasized. No matter how many handsome suitors an ugly millionairess may have, the low social value of ugliness remains a cultural datum. Similarly, the occasional Negro who rises to high social levels cannot be used as an argument against the contention that race is one of the most important ranking principles in Brazilian culture. In the following section an attempt will be made to show the part that race plays in Minas Velhas in the determination of class, and its relative importance in comparison with the other principal determinants of rank.

VII. The most important single diagnostic of class is *wealth*. Among the 1,500 or so persons living in the town of Minas Velhas there are some heads of families who own as much as 600 times more property than others. Annual cash incomes frequently differ by a factor of 10 or more. Houses have from 1 to 20 rooms: some are made of bare adobe, crumbling and near ruin, with packed earth floors and no kitchens, no glass windows and no furniture to speak of; others are elaborately decorated, have wooden floors and ceilings, good kitchens, plenty of latticed glass windows, and are filled with chairs, benches, tables, and a bed for each member of the family. Some women own but one or two dresses, a single undergarment, and no shoes; others have a dozen or more dresses, a score of modern European undergarments, silk stockings and several pairs of shoes and slippers. Men's wardrobes likewise differ enormously in size and quality. These differences in wealth account for substantial differences in everyday behaviour. Some men do not work; some women neither cook, wash clothes or dishes, iron, sew nor carry water, since they can afford servants to do all the normal household drudgery. Wealthy families set their tables with different foods— fresh meats, bread, milk, potatoes and canned goods—which poor families cannot afford. Wealthy men have leisure to enter politics, money to wage campaigns and hold political office, and time and clothes to go to church more often. The rich woman's wardrobe permits her to take part in the evening promenade in the town garden, to attend all the ordinary and special masses in church, and to become a leader in the religious sisterhoods. Rich men travel, know the life of the big cities, and send their children to be educated in colleges and universities. Everything that general opinion considers worth owning or doing is more readily accessible to the rich than the poor. No one in Minas Velhas has ever entertained the slightest notion that there are some things that money cannot buy. 'Money is everything.'

65

Money alone, however, will not take a man to the pinnacle of the social pyramid, even though it will lift him higher than any other single factor. Education has great prestige value also. The more years a man attends school the better he is. Education permits first and most important a mastery of language. The educated speaker attempts to approximate the complexities of written Portuguese, which differs profoundly from the *gíria* (colloquialism) of ordinary people. Long strings of synonyms, full use of the subjunctive and compound tenses and attention to euphony are powerful honorific symbols. The familiarity with uncommon words and erudite grammatical forms automatically bestows an air of distinction upon the speaker and assures him of respect from the uneducated, rich as well as poor. Mere literacy lifts a man above his fellows; the individual who can read and write in the rural zone is sought after not only to decipher letters from distant relatives, but also for advice on everyday affairs.

Occupations likewise show a graded series. Those who are completely dependent upon the strength and endurance of their own physical powers—like the farmers, the water carriers, the woodcutters, etc.—are at the bottom of the list. The artisans whose crafts demand a special skill in addition to sheer physical effort rank slightly higher. Higher still are the storekeepers and commercial travellers who combine a minimum of physical with a certain intellectual effort. Still higher are those who command the labour of others—the landlord farmers who do no work in the fields, and the owners of large workshops who merely supervise production. Those who own large machines like trucks or a flour mill share this level. Owners of special professional monopolies, the doctor, lawyer or dentist who control the destinies and welfare of others, rank still higher. The top place belongs to those who command both the labour and destinies of a large part of the community—the politicians, mayor, councilmen, and political party leaders. For women the bottom place belongs to those who work exclusively with their bodies—fieldhands, water-carriers, washerwomen, woodgatherers, prostitutes, etc. Women with skills like sewing and lacemaking come next. Higher are the housewives, arranged according to how much of the drudgery they have to do themselves. The top position belongs to the schoolteachers and others who have freed themselves completely from household duties. In general, the order is determined by considerations of more or less physical labour, more or less intellectual effort, and more or less control over others.

There are in addition secondary considerations such as family. One's social position tends to be hereditary but only in so far as the diagnostics themselves tend to be self-perpetuating; i.e., children of the rich remain rich, a farmer's son becomes a farmer, children of whites are whites. A child born into a family which has occupied a

5. Street scene in a small town of the Sertão

6. Weaving a basket in Monte Serrat

5. Street scene in a small town of the Sertão

6. Weaving a basket in Monte Serrat

high social level during several generations enjoys only slight intrinsic advantage over the *nouveau riche*. The oldest white families in Minas Velhas are just as liable to be lower as upper class. Deportment, or behaviour viewed morally, is also often taken into account, especially to determine rank within a class, but rarely spells the difference between one class and another.

In order to obtain a representative sample for a standard-of-living survey in Minas Velhas, 100 households were selected on the basis of the occupation of the chief of the household. The number of representatives for each occupation—such as clerks, schoolteachers, ironworkers, etc.—was proportionate to the actual total in the urban population. Using only wealth and occupation as criteria, an upper[1] and a lower[2] group are easily identified in the sample. The upper consists of extremes of wealth either in the form of property or cash income, combined with administrative or executive positions. The lower consists of extremes of poverty combined with menial and unstable occupations—watercarriers, washerwomen, woodcutters, roadworkers, prostitutes, beggars, etc. With but one or two exceptions the boundaries of an upper and lower group so defined stand out in bold relief. Those persons who fit neither into the upper nor the lower can be lumped together for the moment and be regarded as a middle group. The distribution of the sample per 'economic-occupational' group is as follows:

TABLE IV.

	Number of households
Group 'A'	11
Group 'B'	65
Group 'C'	24
TOTAL	100

This table gives us the approximate outline of the urban class structure. The groups designated 'A' and 'C' are for the most part classes in a socio-economic sense. Group 'B', the largest of the three, will be dealt with further on, and for the time being should merely be considered as an aggregate residue. Groups 'A' and 'C' can not only be distinguished on a quantitative basis, but stand out clearly owing to the enormous social distance which separates them. A man from group 'A', with his suit and tie, his umbrella and raincoat, his well-

[1] Property valued above Cr.$50,000.00 and an income higher than Cr.$1,500.00 per month.
[2] No property and a marginal income; i.e., an income sufficient for only a basic subsistence diet—about Cr.$400.00 per month for a non-farming family.

nourished body, his big house, his radio, his knowledge of city life, his important job and his power over others, not only does a thousand things differently from a man in group 'B' or 'C', but he also acts and talks differently with individuals from his own group as compared with the others. People from group 'A' never enter the houses of people in group 'C' and rarely those of group 'B'. They do not become friends with those in group 'C', or if they do it is on a master-servant basis. Their wives do not gossip together, nor go to the same dances; they do not go to the same weddings, funerals, baptisms, etc. Group 'A' controls all the political and economic power. Its members give most of the orders, do least of the work, make the most money and have the most leisure. Group 'C' may be regarded as the servant class, though not all of its members are actually employed as servants for group 'A'. Living on a perpetually marginal basis, these persons consider themselves to be outside the normal social system. With rags for clothes, they cannot even go to church; their children cannot go to school. They appear on the fringe of the religious *festas;* they cannot take part in the processions. With no chairs in their houses they are unable to have visitors. They manage to subsist because their expenses are restricted solely to the purchase of food, and because they have renounced a whole series of what are deemed necessities by the rest of society.

In order to equate these three groups with the real class structure, the two remaining ranking gradients—*education* and *race*—must be combined with those of *wealth* and *occupation*. Are there some individuals (that is, in our sample, heads of families), whose position on the educational or racial gradient is so overwhelmingly good or bad as to put them in a group other than the one they thus far occupy? There is no satisfactory quantitative way in which this question can be answered. We must turn instead to the actual situation and inquire whether there are some individuals who manifest the economic and occupational criteria for a particular group but who reject or are denied full participation in the group for which they seem to qualify. In group 'A' this applies to only one member of our sample. Senhor Waldemar, the Negro councilman, does not belong with the rest despite his wealth and political power.

Waldemar's best friends are in group 'B'. Though he maintains friendly relations with persons in group 'A', the relationship is formal and Waldemar tends to belittle himself. At upper-class parties and dances he keeps in the background. When invited to be seated to have coffee and cake with the rest of the guests, he invariably declines and takes his refeshments standing. No one ever insists too much. The solicitude which is shown him as a councilman in such circumstances depends entirely on the certainty that he will not accept too much of it—that he knows his place, in other words. Though he is invited to most formal upper-class functions, he never visits their houses informally and they never visit his. When his son was married, Waldemar gave a dance. A handful of the *élite* came to congratulate him. They sat around stiffly for a few moments and then one by one took their leave before the party had really got under way. Though well-liked and treated with respect, Waldemar clearly does not 'make the grade'. Because of his colour he is not treated as an equal by the other people in his economic bracket. This fact can be phrased differently: he is not treated as an equal because he is not rich enough or educated enough to overcome being a Negro. If he were the richest man in town (which he is not by far), or if he held a university degree, there is no doubt that he would be taken more seriously.

When the same practical tests are applied to each individual in the second and third groups, it is found that very little change is necessary. Neither race nor education are important enough to effect the transfer over the great social distance which separates these economic-occupational groups. Not more than one or two Negroes at the bottom of group 'B' ought to be shifted to group 'C'. A man who has a steady income, who can afford plates, chairs, shoes, beds and an extra pair of pants is in a class higher than a man who cannot, even though the former is black and the latter is white. Moreover, there are equally few upward jumps from one of these groups to another because a man is white. It can be stated with certainty that *race* and *education* will be significant factors in this incomplete three-part class system only for a negligible number of borderline cases. In the actual sample only two changes are definitely required: the removal

TABLE V.

Gradient	Racial Gradient		
	High White	Medium Mulatto	Low Negro
ECONOMIC			
Average monthly income . .	Cr.$961	Cr.$648	Cr.$445
Average property	Cr.$23,258	Cr.$9,670	Cr.$7,814
EDUCATIONAL			
Literacy	86%	73%	53%
Years of school	3.3 yrs.	2.0 yrs.	1.4 yrs.
Grades completed	2.5	0.87	0.70
OCCUPATIONAL			
Professional-administrative . .	19%	10%	3%
Civil Service and commercial .	22%	13%	7%
Crafts	37%	43%	45%
Menial and agricultural . . .	22%	34%	45%

of one Negro from class 'A' to class 'B', and another from class 'B' to class 'C'. No shifts are required because of *education*.

The failure of the racial gradient to effect a notable modification in this class structure based on economic-occupational criteria does not finally settle the question of the relative importance of racial criteria. We can conclude at this point that economic criteria are more important cues to status than racial criteria, but the method we have been using cannot bring us to any further refinement of the problem. The obstacle in our path is that to a large extent all four gradients are linked together, no matter which gradient is chosen to begin with. This means that having once arranged our sample into high, middle and low economic groups we have already arranged them into high, middle and low occupational, educational and racial groups as well. The extent of this linkage is shown by Table V.

In Table V *race* is taken as the primary gradient, and *education*, *occupation* and *wealth* are shown as its functions. The high degree of correlation[1] explains why a three-class system based only on the economic and occupational gradients is so little modified when race and education are also taken into account.

Table VI shows the distribution of race by class.

TABLE VI

Class	White		Mulatto		Negro		All races	
	No.	%	No.	%	No.	%	No.	%
Class 'A'	9	20	1	4	0	0	10	10
Class 'B'	31	69	14	61	18	60	63	63
Class 'C'	5	11	8	35	12	40	25	25
TOTAL							100[1]	100[1]

[1] Two *caboclos* not shown. The sample consists of the principal wage earner in 100 separate households.

Table VI shows why it is useless to attempt to measure the relative importance of racial criteria *vis-à-vis* other ranking principles by citing a handful of cases concerning Negroes who class higher than whites. The facts are that only 11 per cent of the whites in this *preliminary* class system provide an opportunity for the Negroes to climb above them, and only 60 per cent of the Negroes can take advantage of the opportunity. Hence, the popular adage that 'money whitens' is true but largely irrelevant. It is true that if a Negro in Minas Velhas were vastly wealthy, had a degree in medicine, and was the leader of the *União Democràtica*, he could be a member of

[1] If we proceed on the basis that there is no argument concerning the relative innate abilities of the three racial groups, the reasons for the correlation are obvious enough: the rich inherit from the rich; money buys education, and education is a prerequisite for the best jobs.

group 'A'. Unless this is to be a daydream we must ask: if it is true, then how often does it happen? The answer for Minas Velhas is— once or twice in a lifetime.

The crucial feature of the class structure is the social cleavage which occurs in the middle of group 'B'. It will be remembered that group 'B' was established merely as a statistical residue—the group of persons who fitted into neither group 'A' nor 'C'. A cursory attempt was made to check the lower limits of group 'B' in the light of racial criteria. As a result, one Negro who was right on the economic margin between groups 'B' and group 'C' was transferred to the lower group. This could be done more or less mechanically, because the very concept of class demands a sharper delineation of boundaries than is found in actual fact. Modification in the threefold class structure because of racial criteria would only affect one case in group 'A' and those few doubtful cases which occupied positions astride the margin between group 'B' and 'C', thus the outlines of the three groups would remain essentially unchanged by the broadening of the critique to include all four major ranking gradients. Let us now retrace our steps and consider not merely the outlines of group 'B' but its internal structure.

Within a class, it should be kept in mind, the principle of rank continues to operate. Since group 'B' is such a large one, we can expect to find considerable stratification. As a matter of fact, it is among the members of this economic group that the most profound division in the social structure of Minas Velhas is to be found. Somewhere near the middle of group 'B' one stops talking about whites and begins to talk about Negroes—not as physical types, but as social groups. One of these groups in known in Minas Velhas as *os brancos* (the whites) or *os ricos* (the rich); the other is called *os pretos* (the Negroes) or *os pobres* (the poor). Some additional facts about town life will make this distinction clear.

On the best street, known popularly as *Rua do Clube* (Club Street), the largest and best cared-for building is that of the *Clube Social*—the traditional recreational centre of the city. The *Clube* has a charter granted by the State of Bahia which declares its *raison d'être* as 'Benevolent, Educational and Recreational'. In practice, the *Clube's* charitable efforts are confined largely to an elaborate paperwork scheme of distributing non-existent funds; its educational efforts reside in a dust-shrouded library of about 500 books and pamphlets, most of them in foreign languages; but the *Clube's* recreational function is well exercised. One room is dedicated to a billiard table which is used nightly by the youthful members. Checkers and backgammon are played in another room that contains a radio and a file of Salvador newspapers. In a back room a card game can usually be found in progress. The largest room is reserved for the frequent dances which the *Clube* sponsors, and which are considered the town's most important social events. The *Clube's* president, who is also the State tax collector, is quick to assure visitors that anyone can join. The dues are in fact insignificant but only about one-third of the town's families actually belong. A powerful and thinly disguised selective principle operates to restrict membership. While anyone can join, he must wear a suit and a tie in order to enter the building. More to the point, if anyone can enter the dancing room, it is one of the fundamental axioms of life in Minas Velhas that the girls are very particular whom they will dance with. During the score of dances which were observed at the *Clube* only one Negro—a son of Waldemar—was ever seen on the dance floor. His partner, moreover, was always one of his white sisters-in-law. The rest of the dancers are white or mulatto. These dances provide an excellent opportunity to see who's who. For at every dance those who cannot enter the *Clube*, as well as those who can, make their appearance. The outgroup gathers around in the streets and presses close against the open window of the ballroom, peering in at the proceedings with vaguely wistful eyes. The crowd outside stays there as long as the dance goes on. Sometimes they are as numerous as the dancers. The light which streams out of the ballroom shows most of them to be Negroes. But many mulattoes not much darker than those who are dancing and a handful of whites also appear. If you ask the people inside the *Clube* who the people standing outside are, you will get two interchangeable answers— '*os pobres*' (the poor) and '*os pretos*' (the Negroes). If you ask the people outside who the dancers are, you will get three interchangeable answers: '*os brancos*' (the whites), '*os ricos*' (the rich), and '*gente da alta*' (high-class people).

At this stage the reader ought not to be too upset by the fact that all races are represented in both groups, and yet one group is called 'the whites' and the other 'the Negroes'. This confusion of terms has a sound basis in fact and is not altogether illogical. It does not mean that the people of Minas Velhas cannot distinguish a white from a Negro. It simply means that by and large the people who belong to the *Clube* are white. Those who are not have an excess of money or some other prestige factor in a ratio inversely proportional to their racial 'deficiency'. By and large the group at the window is Negro; those who are not Negroes have a deficiency in money or some other prestige factor inversely proportional to their racial 'excellence'. The 'whites' consist of people with the following characteristics: (a) white and wealthy; (b) white and of average wealth; (c) white and poor; (d) mulatto and wealthy; (e) mulatto and of average wealth; (f) Negro and wealthy.

The 'Negroes' consist of people with these characteristics: (a) white and poverty-stricken; (b) mulatto and poverty-stricken; (c) mulatto and poor; (d) Negro and poverty-stricken; (e) negro and poor; (f) Negro and of average wealth. Approximately 90 per cent of the Negroes, 50 per cent of the mulattoes, and 10 per cent of the whites cannot dance at the *Clube*.

The term 'average wealth' denotes a position in the upper half of group 'B' and the term 'poor' denotes a position in the lower half of group 'B'. Hence, it is clear that group 'B' is not one but two classes, which we may call 'B1' and 'B2', as shown in Figure I.

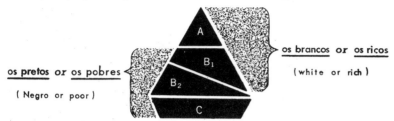

The oblique cleavage in the figure between 'B1' and 'B2' is meant to illustrate the fact that some of the individuals in 'B2' rank higher on the economic, occupational and educational gradients than some of the individuals in 'B1'.

We are now in a position to assess the true significance of race as a criterion of class. While the racial value gradient is not as decisive as the economic gradient, its effect is sufficient to split the middle class in half and to create four classes where only three would otherwise exist.

It is hoped that the attention we have devoted to structural analysis will be regarded by the reader as a necessary background to the proper understanding of an unusually complicated racial situation. Certainly no adequate answer to the questions: is there racial discrimination? or, is there racial prejudice? can be given without relating racial discrimination to class discrimination, or without describing what racial groups are distinguished in the particular society we are studying. From now on the terms *brancos-ricos* (white-rich) and *pretos-pobres* (Negro-poor) will be used as the equivalent of the socially defined 'races'.[1] The fact that only two such racial groups are practically important correlates with the previously noted absence of stereotypes specifically associated with the mulatto.

VIII. Carnival is the high point of the social calendar of Minas Velhas. The traditional centre of fun-making is the *Clube Social*, where highly animated masquerade dances are held on three con-

[1] Actually, of course, this term is a misnomer since the groups which it designates are social classes rather than racial groups. The term is used, for want of a better one, because of the high degree of correlation between upper and white, and lower and Negro.

secutive nights in an atmosphere saturated with intoxicating ether perfume. From time to time the celebrants organize *cordões* and march into the streets where they dance and show off their costumes. Though many whites from distant cities attend and take part in the *Clube's festa*, the *pretos-pobres* of Minas Velhas have never participated. In recent years, the *pretos-pobres* have become increasingly bitter about not being able to enjoy themselves as well as the *brancos-ricos* on this supposedly universal holiday. A small group of political adventurers, *brancos-ricos* but opposed to the ruling clique, saw in the situation an opportunity to create a new political force by championing a separate carnival for the *pretos-pobres*. The proposal of these cynically-motivated power-seekers, many of them members of the *Clube Social*, was enthusiastically supported by a large number of *pretos-pobres*. Few of the latter were aware of the ambitions of their sympathizers, but even if they had been the events which followed would have taken place anyway. As one of the organizers said; 'They have been thinking about this for 20 years, but they (the *pretos-pobres*) were too stupid to do anything about it themselves.' As the scheme gathered momentum its scope became more ambitious. It was decided that a carnival for the *pretos-pobres* was not enough, and that there should be more than one opportunity a year for the non-*Clube* members to enjoy themselves. In the spring of 1948 a mass meeting was held in which plans were made for the organization of a new club that would be a rival to the *Clube Social*. The new club proclaimed itself to be dedicated to 'charitable, recreational and alphabetizing' ends. It was officially named *Sociedade dos Pobres* (Society of the Poor), though it promptly became more popularly known as the *Sociedade dos Pretos*. Plans were made for the approaching carnival and for the construction of a club building. When, to the horror of the *brancos-ricos*, it was suggested that some vacant ground almost next door to the *Clube Social* be purchased as the site of the new edifice, the *pretos-pobres* gleefully dug up the necessary funds. The land was actually purchased, but after the first carnival the activities of the *Sociedade* as well as work on the building languished owing to organizational inexperience and the mounting resistance of the *brancos-ricos*. Three consecutive *preto-pobre* carnivals have been held to date, however, and it is not particularly crucial to the point we are making whether the new club ever gets built or not. Some excerpts from the notes of the *Sociedade's* first meeting may help to show the profundity of the social schism to which the new club owes its origin:

> ...The floor was given to the *orador* (official speechmaker)[1] and he said more or less the following:

[1] The speaker was the leader of the 'Workers' Party of Brazil' (P.T.B.). This party in 1950 won the national elections but was severely defeated in Minas Velhas.

74

'My friends and countrymen! "Society of the Poor"—what a beautiful title! What an attractive name! "He that is humble," says the evangelist, "shall be exalted." This association is really organized by the poor for the poor. But it is necessary to understand fully that the poor with their honest and fertile labour, constitute a richness and a strength which the rich egotist never will be able to destroy.... What a sublime idea inspired the founders of the Association of the Poor! Let us analyse it—"alphabetizing" —that which alphabetizes. This association is created in order to teach the A.B.C. to its members—at least so that they can sign their names.[1] "Recreational"—this association was established in order to provide its members with leisure hours when the cares of life shall be set aside by games, dances, and sambas which are so well loved by all. "Charitable"—this association will create a fund... in order to render aid to those of its members and others who are in need.... The public powers, after learning about our aims will certainly have to give us their support....'

> And so, amid the enthusiastic acclamations of those who no longer are saddened by their humble place and now know that the right to have a club is not the exclusive privilege of the rich, was founded the Association of the Poor.

The *preto-pobre* carnivals have rapidly tended to become more than merely a mechanism for permitting the underprivileged to enjoy themselves. The preparations for carnival are extensive and begin as much as two months before the holiday. Each year a new crop of songs must be learned and many practice sessions (*ensaiadas*) are held in order to make sure that everybody who will take part in the *cordão* will know the words. The *preto-pobre ensaiadas* are performed with an undercurrent of more than casual determination. There is considerable talk of 'bettering' the *brancos-ricos*, i.e., of having the more brilliantly animated celebration. During the actual celebration the *preto-pobre* group leaves the scene of its dance, which is a large house rented for the occasion, and parades past the *Clube Social*. The members of the *cordão* show off their costumes, sing, leap about, and make as much noise and bustle as possible.

Such forms of public rivalry were not absent before the advent of the *preto-pobre* carnival. Two other competitive institutions go back to the beginning of the century. The first has to do with the once religious, but now mainly secular, Festival of the Kings[2] *(Festa dos Reis)*. The festival originally featured a representation of the journey of the Magi to the manger at Bethlehem. Now it is marked by a slow torchlight procession of young girls through the streets. The girls are dressed alike; they dance along slowly in two files singing to the

[1] The speaker here gives himself away. By learning at least to sign their names, they could at least vote in the coming elections.
[2] 'Twelve Nights'.

accompaniment of castanets and musical instruments. They eventually make their way to a predetermined house where the rest of the evening is given over to the usual ballroom dancing. Each year the procession has a different theme which is expressed by the costumes and the songs. In Minas Velhas the girls who participate are all either *pretas-pobres* or *brancas-ricas*. Some years two different *festas* are held simultaneously; the rest of the time, depending on who takes the initiative, only one group or the other may perform the celebration. Strong emphasis is placed on perfecting the costumes and the procession so that the *Reis das Pretas* may be better than the *Reis das Brancas*.

Another focus of rivalry is the town band. From about 1910 to 1940 there were two *filarmônicas* in Minas Velhas. One was associated with the *Clube Social*, the other with the now defunct religious Brotherhood of Rosario *(Irmandade do Rosário)*, which was also known as the 'Brotherhood of the Negroes'. When the Church of Rosário fell into ruin and had to be demolished the Brotherhood disbanded, leaving the musicians on their own. For a while the *Clube's* band was dominant; then in 1922 the *preto-pobre* musicians reorganized, and started the 'Artisan's Lyre'. A period of intense competition ensued, with each organization trying to outdo the other in splendour of uniforms and instruments. The *Clube* even went so far as to hire a professional musician to train replacements; when the music master died, however, the *Clube's* band slowly deteriorated, and for the moment the 'Lyre' reigns supreme.

The Brotherhood of Rosário itself was an interesting example of the racial schism. It existed contemporaneously with a 'white' brotherhood. Its leaders were white, but the rank and file were Negroes. A dispute between the treasurer and the caretaker of the church involved the priest, who sided with the caretaker. The squabble had a political as well as a racial and class background in much the same way as was later true of the *Sociedade dos Pobres*. While the bickering went on the church began to leak and finally the walls collapsed, ending the argument.

Another example is the *festa* of São Sebastião. For 75 years the organization of this holiday has been confined to members of a single Negro family, for whom São Sebastião is the chief saint in the household pantheon. It has become known as a *festa dos pretos*, though *brancos-ricos* attend the special mass and bid in the auction which is an important feature of all such religious celebrations. The presence of a large number of whites at last year's auction elicited the following comment from one of the Negro organizers: 'They (the *brancos-ricos*) don't let us go to their *festas*, and when we have ours they butt in so much that they seem to be the owners.'

It must be admitted, however, that such examples of occasions or institutions which are duplicated because of the class-race differ-

76

ential are not very numerous. This does not detract from the enormous differences in the behaviour of the respective classes, nor from the intensity of the emotions connected with those few instances in which the racial factor is clearly the dominant one. There are great differences between the classes in Minas Velhas, but inter-class tension is mostly restricted to the area close to the narrow margin between *brancos* and *pretos*. There is no possibility of tension between class 'A' and class 'C', or class 'B' and class 'C', even though both different economic and racial groups are involved. There can be no tension precisely because these differences are all so great. To imagine that the situation we have been describing is an instance of an economically-based general 'class struggle' would be a severe distortion of the facts. There is no sense of oppression in class 'B' or class 'C', because the fundamental justice and correctness of the principle of rank and of the major ranking gradients are believed in by all members of the community. Nothing in Minas Velhas is more stable and more tenacious than the belief that some people are better than others, and that the best deserve and get the best. The number of institutions which seem to express inter-class tension are limited precisely because the bone of contention is not the principle of rank, but how that principle is interpreted on a particular level of the hierarchy, namely between classes 'B1' and 'B2'. Here the economic differential is insignificant; indeed, from a purely economic point of view, group 'B' is but a single class. The tension arises exactly because of the essential lack of difference between the two groups. The Negroes in 'B2' seek not to destroy or level the class above them; they seek to enter it. They are prevented from doing this not because of an economic but because of a racial factor. What is at stake is the relative importance of the racial ranking gradient. The whites tend to exaggerate it and the Negroes tend to minimize it. Hence there is no justification for dismissing racial discrimination as a chimerical side-effect of the class structure. Some of the whites want two grades where some of the Negroes think only one should exist. The white girls, by refusing to dance with the Negroes at the *Clube Social* and other formal dances, force the issue. The normally-educated, self-supporting, well-dressed Negroes cannot take part in the life of what they feel is their social level. They are discriminated against and they do not like it. In this limited but vital sense, genuine racial tension exists in Minas Velhas.

It is the Negro of 'average wealth' whose feelings are most impassioned, and whose actions are likely to be most militant, over the genuine racial barrier which excludes him from the white man's domain. He is part of the large group of artisans who in their small-scale home workshops are all limited by an almost primitive machineless technology to the same meagre level of production. Their tools are the same, their skills equal, they make the same products;

yet some of them can dance in the *Clube Social* and others cannot. Sebastiana, for example, is a Negress and a highly skilled iron worker. She owns her own home forge and turns out stirrup frames which are in constant demand. Sebastiana has a reputation for being one of the more outspoken critics of the *brancos-ricos*, and often takes the initiative in organizing the *Reis dos Pretos*. 'People say that I want to be better than the whites,' she says. 'But it isn't that. I am the mistress of my life. I know just what I do. I have my work just like they have, my craft just like they have, so why are they better than I am?' Six months after making this statement, and by way of proving it, Sebastiana married a white man. The man had no profession and no steady income, and she had to set about teaching him to be a blacksmith. Thus it was not all the whites with whom she was angry, but only those who claimed they were better than she was and had no right to do so.

Sebastiana's attitude contrasts strongly with the attitude of Negroes in class 'C'. The latter are placed in few situations where race has crucial ranking value. Thus José, a poor Negro sharecropper, declares: 'The white people of Minas Velhas treat us nicely. They don't call us buzzards or *negros*. Dona Autélia (wife of the town's wealthiest landowner) gave my wife a dress once. She's a great lady.'

We may expect racial tension at any point where, all other factors being equal, the Negro is treated in a manner which is incompatible with his own opinion of the relative importance of the racial ranking gradient. This situation is most likely to occur, as we have said, in the middle group. It is unlikely to occur in the upper class because there are so few Negroes; it is equally unlikely to occur in the lower group because there are so few whites.

An instance of racial tension in the lower class can be cited, however, which has deep significance. Since 1940 the county of Minas Velhas, with State and federal aid, has undertaken a programme of expanding school facilities in the remote rural areas. Schools were created in almost all of the large farming 'satellites'—with the exception of Baixa de Gambá, the all-Negro group of sharecroppers some 10 miles outside of town. Whereas, before the beginning of the expansion, these rural clusters considered schools to be a luxury which they could not afford and to which they had no right, it now became apparent that they were entitled to them. The people of Baixa de Gambá began to clamour for what had become the normal due of sharecroppers, and which apparently they were being denied simply because they were Negroes. Sr. Waldemar undertook to champion their cause. Some excerpts from a speech of his to the Municipal Council will help to illustrate the issues which were involved:

Mr. President, I asked for the floor in order to bring to the attention of this House the visit I made to the new Municipal School of Baixa de Gambá... I still don't know... why this House did not receive with favour my project to establish a school in Baixa de Gambá... even though after much debate and discussion it was approved.... But even after that crisis was passed and the project was approved, there appeared another and still greater one. The functioning of the school remained forgotten. This perhaps because a teacher wasn't found right away... but I believe that only one cause existed, namely that the village of Baixa de Gambá is inhabited by Negroes. But as Negroes they also have the right to learn to read and write, since, Mr. President, the Negro is also one of God's children...

(Now that the school has finally begun to function) we can see that the Negroes of Baixa de Gambá really do have the desire to read and write. The school will enable them later on to bring products more important than firewood and straw to our market, since the principal gate to progress for a people is education. From the (large) attendance at the school we see that the Negroes of Baixa de Gambá have a desire for good things despite the financial situation with which they are afflicted...

The tendency for the white to rate the Negro lower than the Negro rates himself is universal, but the issue is obscured by the greater difference in behaviour due to position in the economic gradient. Even in the lower class, however, as in the case of the school for Baixa de Gambá, a disturbing phantom sometimes swims into view. Class in Minas Velhas is like a heavy muffling cloak; whenever it can momentarily be set aside, very disquieting murmurs of protest can be heard. Whether or not this means that beneath the weight of the class hierarchy there lie buried the seeds of racial unrest, we shall attempt to answer in the next section. Meanwhile let us summarize the main features of inter-racial relations in Minas Velhas:

1. The implications of the racial ranking gradient and of the racial stereotypes are only partially fulfilled in actual behaviour.
2. Race is secondary to economics as a diagnostic of rank.
3. Race, economics, occupation and education are linked in such a way that most Negroes would be in the lower strata of society even if racial differences were unimportant.
4. Nonetheless, in the large middle section of the social hierarchy race is used to split a single economic bracket in half.
5. This split is contested by Negroes and mulattoes whose rank by other criteria ought to be equal or higher.
6. The Negroes have attempted to duplicate certain institutions from which they have been excluded.
7. These institutions are in themselves limited and relatively unimportant today, but there is no doubt that they are concrete expressions of inter-racial tension.

8. From time to time inter-racial tensions also appear outside the middle class, but the modes by which these tensions are expressed are non-violent and mainly verbal.

IX. Serious attention should be devoted to the possibility that the future may bring more militant and widespread racial tension to Minas Velhas. Of course, even if there were no real racial discrimination in actual behaviour, the existence of stereotypes as invidious as the ones we have cited can scarcely be regarded as an indication of a society without 'racial' antagonisms. But we have seen that the gap between ideal and actual patterns associated with race comes very near to being bridged when the physically-defined Negro group is replaced by the socially-defined 'Negro-poor' group. The socially-defined 'Negro-poor' is actually treated as an inferior, though for the most part the treatment might be dismissed (wrongly enough) as the mere expression of class differences.

Minas Velhas, with its emphasis on home industry and its large artisan class, is not a wholly typical Brazilian town. This very 'atypicality', however, may indicate a trend to be expected in rural Brazil. From the point of view of race and class relations, the development of home crafts has meant that an unusually heavy concentration of Negroes and mulattoes is to be found in the same economic brackets which the whites occupy. The whites, on the average, still enjoy by far a higher standard of living than the Negroes, but more Negroes than is normal for Brazil can match them. The normal synchronism between the racial value gradient and the economic value gradient is threatened to a considerable extent; the white finds a large number of Negroes placed higher than they should be, and tries to restore the balance which is called for by the ideal stereotypes. While there is still no absolute prohibition against Negroes occupying positions equal to or higher than the whites, there is a definite limit to the number whom the whites can safely permit to do so. This number or 'quota' is determined by the imponderable but certainly finite extent to which the gap between ideal and actual behaviour may be stretched. For the more Negroes that the white must accept in the 'white-rich' class, the more difficult it becomes for him to profess the absolute dispraisal required by the stereotypes, together with the principle that 'money whitens'. Hence the more Negroes that money actually does 'whiten', the more money is required for that whitening to take place. As the gap between the whites' wished-for social hierarchy and the real social hierarchy tends to increase, so too does the relative importance of race as a criterion of class tend to increase. An increasing number of Negroes find themselves denied participation of their level of the hierarchy simply because they are Negroes. The bitterness and ill-will generated by this exclusion are expressed by duplicative and competitive institutions such as the two clubs, the two bands, the two brotherhoods, and the two *Festas dos Reis*. Though the duplication is thus far restricted to a relatively minor list of institutions, there is a definite trend in that direction. In effect, if the vertical cleavage between the 'white-rich' and the 'Negro-poor' is allowed to extend itself unchecked, the duplicate institutions may very well multiply to such an extent that the community will split in half and give birth to a caste society.

It is obvious that any substantial rise in the general standard of living in the near future will increase this danger. Such a rise must begin by reducing the enormous group of marginal, illiterate and poverty-stricken persons in the lower socio-economic group, almost 90 per cent of whom are of mixed racial descent. Both by direct administrative efforts and as the result of an historical process which is taking place in all the underdeveloped regions of the world, the marginal and sub-marginal class in Brazil is slowly but steadily diminishing while the middle class grows larger. Consciously or unconsciously, this progress is essentially the progress of a racial minority which but 75 years ago was an enslaved group. As universal education and higher wages for menial labour become available to the under-privileged groups, the cleavage between the upper and lower social classes might be expected to include at least occupational discrimination. Certainly, by the sheer increase in the number of persons involved in the disputed levels of the class hierarchy, there is a possibility that racial tension will increase.

BIBLIOGRAPHY

1. Lima (1944), p. 69.
2. James (1942), p. 442.
3. Calmon (1935), p. 93.

RACE RELATIONS IN THE ARID SERTÃO¹

by
BEN ZIMMERMAN

I. A vast area of north-eastern Brazil, which includes the States of Ceará, Rio Grande do Norte, Paraíba, large parts of Pernambuco, Piauí and Bahia and smaller sections of Alagoas and Sergipe, is an arid semi-desert. In altitude it rises from a few hundred feet above sea level in Ceará to 1,000–1,500 feet in northern Bahia. Occasionally, there is a low mountain; for the most part, however, it is an arid plain, covered with *caatinga* (literally, white bush) which somewhat resembles the scrub-brush vegetation of Texas. Although the word *sertão* may be defined as 'interior', 'backlands', or 'hinterland'—and, thus, is often used by Brazilians to mean any part of their country which is inland from the coast—this particular *sertão* has assumed a special significance in Brazil. It is this region which is struck periodically by droughts; it is here that there have been occasional outbursts of religious fanaticism which have sometimes taken the form of revolutionary (or counter-revolutionary) movements. The *sertanejo*, as the inhabitant of this region is called, is often looked upon as having a special character. As described by Euclides da Cunha, the Brazilian writer whose powerful study of this area, *Os Sertões*,² was published at the end of the last century, the *sertanejo* is noted for his unmitigated dourness, a circumspection that can amount to a total lack of trust, for periods of extreme lassitude which he alternates with bursts of violent activity. The geographer Preston James, has emphasized the mysticism of the area: the *sertão* is 'a state of mind, a belief in the existence of hidden resources, and the story of a people endowed with unusual insights and powers, [1].³

No one knows with any certainty the number of Indians who lived in the north-east before the Portuguese began colonizing Brazil. The quality of the soil, which is difficult to work even with the iron tools now available, would seem to militate against a heavy concentration of population in aboriginal times. Ethnographic evidence, on the other hand, suggests that Indian influence may have been considerable: the vegetation is often called by Indian or Indian-derived names; the map is literally dotted with place-names, many of which are of Indian origin; several cities in the north-east, such as Natuba and Itapicuru, developed from Jesuit- or Franciscan-sponsored mission villages. It is often said, in some of the communities,

¹ Field-work on which this paper is based lasted from July 1950 to June of the following year. It was sponsored jointly by the State of Bahia and Columbia University, with additional funds from the Area Research Training programme of the Social Science Research Council. During various periods, I was assisted in the field by Lincoln Allison Pope and Nilda Guerra de Macêdo who have put their field notes at my disposal and to whom I wish to express my very great appreciation.
² This book is available in English under the title *Revolt in the Backlands*, translated by Samuel Putnam (University of Chicago, 1944).
³ The figures in brackets refer to the bibliography on page 113.

that the forbears of the residents were 'wild Indians of the forest' (*indios brabos do mato*) who were captured with the aid of fierce dogs. The greatest evidence for an Indian background, however, comes from the physical type, which is predominantly *caboclo*, the result of the Indian crossed with European whites of the Mediterranean variety. Many people display the epicanthic fold or the straight, coarse, black hair which is associated with the Mongoloid races.

The Europeans, also, were far from numerous in the beginning. During the early part of the sixteenth century, the only interest of the Portuguese in north Brazil was in Brazilwoods,[1] the dyewoods which were so ardently sought after during the Middle Ages [2]. A little later, settlers moved to the interior from the towns and cities of the sugar region. The first sections which were thus occupied were in Ceará, inland from the capital city of Fortaleza and along the lower and middle course of the São Francisco river in Bahia [3]. Grazing became the chief economic activity; and, from the beginning, the owners of the *fazendas* (ranches) resented interference from the coast or even from Portugal, since they were using the land with little regard to property lines [4]. Their isolation was officially enforced by royal charters and decrees. Migration to the area was severely restricted. As a consequence of these circumstances, the north-east became a refuge for assassins, vagabonds and adventurers, and the *fazendeiro* (rancher) with his armed bands of retainers a familiar figure in the *sertão*.

Negroes, likewise, appear to have been relatively few in number. In a region that was essentially pastoral, a concentration of slaves as in the plantation economy of the 'sugar coast' would not be found. In one municipality a total of 533 slaves were registered for freedom in 1885; a decade earlier, 538 slaves were mentioned. For the most part, the slaves were engaged in *lavoura* (agriculture) if they were men, and in domestic service if women. Towards the end of the nineteenth century, a number were employed in more skilled occupations such as dressmaking or tailoring, and some few were even *vaqueiros* (cowboys). It should be noted that in the lists of slaves registered for freedom, very few are identified as *preto*; a majority are described as *cabra*, a designation which suggests that they were already mixed. The proportion of Negroes, therefore, was very much the same as today: numerically speaking, they have always been a peripheral element in the *sertão*.

Like most regions of Brazil, the north-east had its flourishing period. This occurred in the late seventeenth and early eighteenth century with the discovery of the gold and diamond mines in Minas Gerais, and coincided with the decline of the 'sugar coast'. Plantation owners and their slaves began to move south on the São Francisco river. The *sertanejos* provided them with food and supplies for

---

[1] The area used for collection of Brazilwood was mainly along the coast.

83

the long journey and often acted as guides to the mining area. Large urban concentrations, however, have never been typical of the *sertão*. About 85 per cent of the population is rural. Although pastoralism has, in recent years, given way to agriculture, the *vaqueiro* is still looked upon in many ways as the typical resident of the area.

The aspects of the *sertão* which have most captured the imagination of writers are the droughts and the fanatics with which the area is identified.

The picture of the north-east, however, as a cul-de-sac filled with fanatics and bandits of one sort or another, has changed considerably. Highways have been cut through the arid soil, and in countless ways the zone is being brought into the national life. Many people, especially of the intellectual and commercial classes, are eager to dissociate themselves from what they consider to be an unworthy impression of their area. They bitterly resent the stereotype with which they have become identified. As in Joazeiro do Norte, they point proudly to their new hospital, their commercial school, their more than 100 *oficinas* of goldworkers. In other respects, however, the change has been less striking. People still tend to be adventurers, eager to get rich by a *golpe* or coup. Authority is so greatly resented that a public official could say: 'Do you think I would call the police if I were robbed? Not I! I'd take care of the criminal myself!'

II. The community of Monte Serrat is at the southern tip of this huge area. It is part of the municipality with which it shares its name and includes, for the purposes of this paper, the city of Monte Serrat and the rural districts with which it is associated.[1] The community falls naturally into a number of zones. At the centre is the city of Monte Serrat. It is here that the more affluent members of the community live, and that people come to conduct their business or to attend an important Mass. Beyond this, to the distance of about three leagues,[2] the land is devoted almost entirely to the production of food crops, much of which is brought to the weekly fair for sale to the urban residents. The first cattle ranches appear at the northern and eastern extremities of this zone and extend to a region known as the *alto-sertão*, which is considerably more arid than Monte Serrat and where commercial food production has been almost entirely replaced by subsistence farming. This situation is indicated in Figure I. Except in the city, settlement tends to be of the scattered type. Even on a *fazenda* where all the families are related, there is often a distance of a kilometre or more between dwellings. At the

[1] Since Monte Serrat is a city (or administrative seat), a community as well as a municipality, care will be taken throughout to identify which unit is under consideration.
[2] A league is six kilometres or about four miles.

84

present time, the city has a population of about 1,600; the rural districts have perhaps three times that number. For the most part, the people are of the *caboclo* racial type, that is a blend of Indian and white. About 10 per cent are definitely causasoid, while a slightly smaller percentage are either Negro or mulatto.

Despite the important bonds which unite the urban and rural populations, there are equally strong elements which divide them.

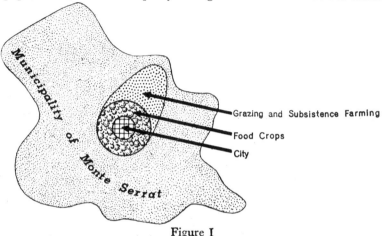

Grazing and Subsistence Farming

Food Crops

City

Figure I

City people refer to the rural people as *caatingueiros*, *tabareus*, or, sometimes more gently, *o povo do mato*—the people who live in the woods. All these terms are in varying degrees opprobrious and suggest that the rural people are ungainly, stupid, and lacking in those graces which city people find acceptable. A common expression, often uttered humorously, is: *'Que acha? O tabareu é gente?'* Literally translated, this means: 'What do you think? Are yokels people?' A woman remembers the time when the *tabareus*, on arriving in the city, led their burros into the parlours of the houses. Rural people often retaliate by calling city folk snobbish or *granfinos*—arrogant dandies. The chief reason for deriding the rural population is that most of them work as *roceiros* of farmers, and a *roceiro* by definition is lower-class. It is not uncommon, however, for city people of the lower class to identify themselves with the rural dwellers. Once when an important official criticized the rural people who had sponsored a dance during a solemn holiday by calling them *tabareus* and accusing them of lack of manners—a serious criticism in a society where people are expected to know their place—the lower-class people of the city were indignant and threatened to sponsor a dance themselves in order to retaliate.

The rural-urban dichotomy is indeed, in many ways, a more important criterion than race in determining the class position of an individual. A light person who is a *roceiro* would be considered lower-class almost to the same degree as a dark person who was engaged in a similar occupation. At the same time, not all people who live in the rural areas can be considered equal in status. Relatives of important families in the city often work in the *caatingas*—generally as overseers of the family property—and they, like their kin in the city, would be accepted as upper-class. The great majority of upper-class people, however, live in the city and, if they have rural properties, they hold them as absentee landlords. As with so many other aspects of this society, the criteria for class membership are changing. It is still true, however, that the most important attribute for upper-class membership is family background or, as the people of Monte Serrat put it, *antecedentes*. There are no families in the community who are descended from the 'great' families of Brazil, such as the Calmões, the Prados, the Wanderleys and others who constitute an unofficial nobility. Within the community, however, the families are carefully rated and to identify one's self with one of them is a way of gaining prestige. In the rural zone, it is not uncommon for a person to say that he is a cousin in some remote degree to the Cardozos, the most important and numerically the largest family in the municipality. It is likewise not uncommon for the city-dwelling members of this family to trace their ancestry as far back as the original owner of the Fazenda Araça, from whom they actually are descended. One of the reasons, in fact, that a Negro can never truly be upper-class in the community is because he does not have a 'family', a point which will be made clearer shortly.

Within recent years another criterion of status has become as important as family: money. So far as most the people in the community are concerned, this is now the only one of any real importance. They point, as an example, to one of the leading families who, until a short time ago, would not allow their children to marry any one who was not of an equally good family and also *formado*—that is, with a professional degree. Now the daughters of the head of this family are engaged to men who are becoming important in the commercial life of the community. Neither of these men is particularly well-educated and the family of one of them is noted for its bad manners and violence. What has made him acceptable as son-in-law is the fact that his brother is the leading *comerciante* in the community, who owns several *depósitos* or warehouses, has a fleet of four trucks, and is the most important dealer in sisal which he purchases and transports for re-sale in the larger cities where he has important credit connexions. Even people who are ill-disposed to this *comerciante* point out that he will, no doubt, make the next 'fortune' in the municipality.[1] Many people view the changes which have been taking place

[1] 'Fortune' is a relative term. There are no people of great wealth in Monte Serrat.

with wistfulness or with bitterness. '*Aqui só vale que tem*,' they say: 'Here what is valued is what one has.' It is likely that this proverb at one time referred to family connexions; new people relate it only to money.

The determination of a person's class position is, broadly speaking, the result of a combination of these two factors. Depending upon the point of view, there are three, four, or, possibly, only two classes in Monte Serrat. The people themselves normally recognize only two: *os bons*, a phrase which might be translated by the slang expression, 'the big shots', and *os pobres*, or the poor people. *Os bons* would include the *fazendeiros* of 'good family', the more important government officials, such as the judge and the district attorney, and those *comerciantes* who have managed to attain influential positions in the community. *Os pobres* would automatically include everyone else, the *roceiros*, the artisans, the menials and the less affluent commercial people. Some people, however, feel there is no upper-class in Monte Serrat. 'We are all poor here', a man once stated categorically. A schoolteacher, on the other hand, herself of 'good family', felt that there was a rather large middle-class and the people of Monte Serrat, in unguarded moments, speak of people who are *mais ou menos* (more or less) or *remediado*. In this group would fall many of the artisans, a number of the *comerciantes*, and the smaller Government employees. A fourth group, relatively small in size, might also be identified. These are the people referred to as the *coitados* who are, in a certain sense, almost outside the class structure: beggars, prostitutes, the extremely aged or infirm. These people have become the responsibility of the entire group. They are helped with alms, with food, and with money collected by the religious brotherhoods and one prefaces almost all references to any of them with the adjective, *coitado*—the poor thing.

In terms of social stratification, however, these various classes may be consolidated. There is a point beyond which a number of people who might be considered *mais ou menos* ordinarily do not reach. If they are *comerciantes* or artisans, they depend for their trade on the lower-class people of the city and the *caatingas*. They are rarely invited—or would think of going unasked—to *festas* sponsored by people who are above them in the social scale. Their identification in personal as well as social terms is with the *pobres*. Another part of this group, however, maintains extremely close relations with the upper class. They are friends or political and commercial associates of the *bons*. From this point of view, the division of the society into two large, though unequal, groups has a certain validity. This situation is illustrated in Figure II. The groups are divided into three classes. A heavy line indicates the point of division in terms of social stratification. The *coitados* are included with the lower class, though separated by a dotted line. The percentages indicate the estimated number of people in each segment.

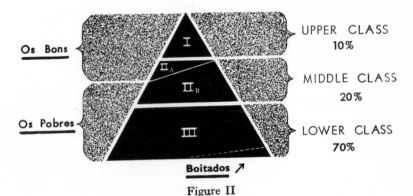

Figure II

With the exception of the Negro, people of all racial types may be found in all classes. The lightest people, however, are concentrated in the upper class, while the majority of the darker people fall in the two lower groups. This becomes especially apparent in terms of occupation. Government employees, for example, because of the money, education and personal influence required to obtain these positions are preponderantly white and upper-class. Shopkeepers, on the other hand, are mainly of the darker races, though most often *caboclo* and middle-class.[1] Except for unusual circumstances, which will be discussed in another section of this paper, Negroes and mulattoes are all lower-class and occupy rather menial positions. In Table I the 35 adult mulattoes and the 19 Negroes in the city of Monte Serrat are listed according to occupation, race and sex.

The exclusion of the Negro from the upper-class in Monte Serrat is due primarily, of course, to the circumstance that there are few Negroes in the community.[2] However, even were the number of Negroes greater, it is unlikely that any of them would have risen appreciably in the social scale. The reason most often given for this is that Negroes are descendants of slaves, bearing the physical marks of their ancestry, and are consequently without one of the most important attributes of social status in the community: good family. There is even a saying to the effect that *'quem é de família são os brancos'*—people who belong are the whites. Poorer people, conversely, are often said to be *sem importancia*—that is, without importance so far as 'Society' is concerned. In the case of the Negroes it is often specifically pointed out that this is because they 'have no relatives' (*parentes*) and thus cannot amount to much.

In fantasy, it is true, Negroes sometimes surpass the whites, as it happens in folklore where the poor boy who becomes wealthy and marries the princess is represented by a negro youth.

[1] See Appendix I for a detailed listing of these groups.
[2] Most of the Negroes in the municipality do not live in the community of Monte Serrat.

In real life, also, a Negro occasionally becomes important in 'Society'. People speak of a Negro *promotor* (district attorney) who was once stationed in Monte Serrat: 'He was admitted to all the social functions.' They point out, however, that he was *de fora*—that is, an outsider and not a 'child of here', and that he was an educated man. The degree to which he was accepted by the upper class, however, is another matter. A young woman, speaking of him, said that he once asked her to dance at a *festa*. She wanted not to because of his *qualidade*, but since he was a *promotor* she felt she could not refuse.

Despite the strong class divisions, what often militates against open hostility, is the extraordinary warmth which characterizes personal relations. In part this is due to the vast extension of the family.

TABLE I.

Occupation	Women		Men	
	Mulatto	Negro	Mulatto	Negro
Maid	9	3	—	—
Dressmaker	2	1	—	—
Water carrier	5	2	—	—
Midwife	1	—	—	—
Prostitute	1	—	—	—
Candy-maker	—	1	—	—
Chauffeur	—	—	2	2
Musician	—	—	—	1
Shoemaker	—	—	4	3
Field hand	—	—	2	2
Shopkeeper	—	—	1	—
Soldier	—	—	1	—
Announcer on public address system	—	—	1	—
Public functionary	—	—	1	—
Unemployed	4	—	1	4

People speak of themselves as being one great family, and in a certain sense this is true. Family relationships have been strengthened and augmented through such devices as the *compadre* system by which, at various crises in life such as baptism or confirmation, or on specific ceremonial occasions such as the Eve of St. John's Day, one acquires godparents and godchildren. Adoption of children is exceedingly frequent and though, in most cases, people tend to adopt children of their relatives, it is not unusual for a family to bring up the children of an acquaintance or even a stranger. Immigration into the area has been slight and when it has occurred has also tended to follow family connexions: a person will move to Monte Serrat because he already has actual or ceremonial relatives living there. It is possible, therefore, that all the people may be in some degree related. Within the limits of the city, however, people of the lower class are careful not to mention publicly their connexion with the more important families. They are expected to remain within their class, or they may incur the hostility of the more affluent members of the community.

Equally important with the extended family, however, is the concept of *amizade* which may be defined as friendship, although it is more than that. It includes the concepts of responsibility and obligation, so that every favour a person receives must be returned. Sometimes, the favours follow a vertical pattern, and it is not uncommon for a person of the lower class to offer his services without charge to a person of the upper class who has befriended him. On other occasions, it may include an exchange between equivalents: a *roceiro* may assist a friend during his harvest expecting that when he is ready to collect his crops the service will be returned. A person who finds himself in difficulty may rely upon his friends to be his *coiteiros*, and the fierce loyalty for which the area is noted is partly due to the principle of *amizade*. It was this aspect of the culture that an upper-class woman was thinking of when she said: '*Aqui nós moramos juntos*'—here, we all live together.

III. In order to comprehend the background of race relations in Monte Serrat, it is important to remember that the culture of the community is the result of the interaction of three relatively distinct historical traditions—the native or Indian, the African and the European. Traces of these traditions are apparent in almost every aspect of the culture; at the same time, the influences of each of the three traditions is stronger in some directions than in others. Except in physical type, which has already been mentioned, Indian influence appears to be rather slight.

A few traits associated with the economic life are derived from the aboriginal peoples.

There are, likewise, few traits in the culture which are truly African. It is possible that, apart from some of the tales, other folklore elements such as some of the riddles with which the people of Monte Serrat entertain themselves, are also African. These riddles are often cast as elaborate puns and generally start with the question, '*O quê que é?*' (What is it)? A system of work parties which existed in Monte Serrat until recently may also, in part, have been adapted from a similar pattern in Africa.

It is in practices associated with religion that African influence is most marked. Like most Brazilians, the people of Monte Serrat are

7. Children of Monte Serrat

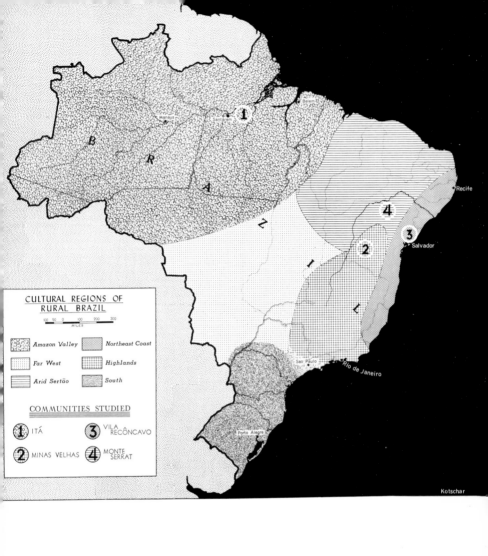

CULTURAL REGIONS OF
RURAL BRAZIL

100 50 0   100   200   300
              MILES

Amazon Valley   Northeast Coast

Far West   Highlands

Arid Sertão   South

COMMUNITIES STUDIED

1 ITÁ   3 VILA RECÔNCAVO

2 MINAS VELHAS   4 MONTE SERRAT

Kotschar

7. Children of Monte Serrat

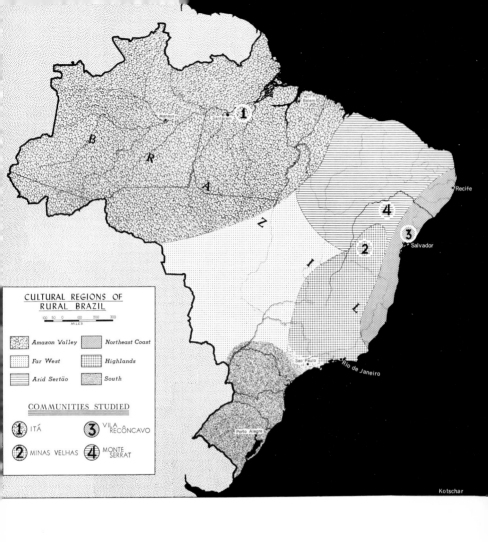

CULTURAL REGIONS OF
RURAL BRAZIL

100 50 0   100   200   300
MILES

Amazon Valley   Northeast Coast

Far West   Highlands

Arid Sertão   South

COMMUNITIES STUDIED

1 ITÁ   3 VILA
                     RECÔNCAVO

2 MINAS VELHAS   4 MONTE
                     SERRAT

Manaus
Belém
Santarém
Recife
Salvador
São Paulo
Rio de Janeiro
Porto Alegre

Kotschar

Catholics and, with the rest of the country, share certain re-interpretations of Catholic doctrine. The 'cult of the saints'—that is, devotion to a particular saint—is greatly developed, as is the 'cult of Mary'. In many Brazilian towns, the devotion of the people is to the patron saint of the community; in Monte Serrat, however, though a majority of the houses have a picture of the Sacred Heart of Jesus, almost everyone has selected a private saint with whom he is, almost literally, on speaking terms. The relationship between the devotee and the saint is extremely personal. The devotee asks the saint for favours, assuming, in return, certain obligations. A person may say: '*Meu Santo Antonio* (My Saint Anthony), if I return safely from this trip, I will offer candles at your altar.' Only if the person returns safely does he have to carry through his part of the bargain—and without delay, for any untoward procrastination will *aborecer* the saint, that is, annoy him. The saints, in this respect, are looked upon as personal servants who must, when called upon by their devotees, do as they are asked.

Another aspect of the 'people's religion' concerns certain magical practices. The city, as well as the rural area, is filled with *rezadores* or people who pray. These *rezadores* treat people for various ailments, some of them real ones such as rheumatism or worms, but also for illnesses which are due to the evil eye. The evil eye is a quality, though a treacherous one, which a person has and can do nothing about. If a person with such eyes looks at a child, particularly a pretty child, the child is apt to die. If he looks at leaves they are likely to wither. There is said to be a man in a community to the north of Monte Serrat who always walks with downcast eyes for this reason. People sometimes become ill because someone has given them the evil eye. Radios (of which there are 14 in Monte Serrat) sometimes cease operating for the same reason. The person with this abominable quality is not looked upon as vicious since this capacity was wished upon him. The person whom the evil eye attacks, however, can call a *rezador*, and be treated by prayers which the *rezador* has learned, generally from other *rezadores* and, less frequently, from printed manuals. Other ways of avoiding the evil eye are to wear a *figa*, a charm consisting of a clenched fist with a protruding thumb; to place a cow's skull on the fence surrounding a field; to drop bulls' horns in the fields or to place them on the shelves of shops.

A specifically African institution into which the complex of spirits, both good and bad, has entered is *candomblé*, the term used for the Negro fetish cults of Salvador. *Candomblé*, or *terreiro*, which is the more common name in Monte Serrat, is a religious cult in which the adherents become possessed by any one of a number of 'saints'. Many of these 'saints' have a Catholic counterpart: Saint Barbara is known in the *terreiro* as Xangó or, less frequently, as

Nagé; Saint Roche is Omolú; our Lord of the Good End (Senhor do Bonfim) is Oxalá; Saint Anthony is Ogun. In addition, there are a number of Indian 'saints' who have no corollary in the Catholic hierarchy, such as Tapuya and Tupinambá. Each of the 'saints' has a special costume and symbols of its power, as well as a 'voice' by which it speaks through the people it has possessed. The 'saint' makes itself evident by entering the head of its children (*filhos)* and riding them (literally, mounting them). The *filhos* then spend hours dancing, after which they can recall nothing of what has happened: for the time being, they have become the 'saint'. In Monte Serrat, this institution has undergone significant changes; there it must be looked upon basically as a curing society. The primary function of the cult in Monte Serrat is to relieve people of the *encosta* (the intrusive) or *caboclo* which has made them ill— which is but one of the many functions of the *candomblé* cults of the city of Salvador.

There are said to be six *mães* and *pais de santo* in this municipality (literally, mothers or fathers of the saint).[1] Within the limits of the city, 'the drums are no longer beaten'. But a few leagues from Monte Serrat, in a rural area, the most famous *mãe de santo* operates her cult. This woman also works as a *curador* or curer. People suffering from whatever ailment may come to her for treatment. Her first treatment generally consists of prayers, a number of baths (always an odd number) as well as prescriptions for certain medicines *do mato* (of the woods), again an odd number. After this, if the treatment has not shown the desired effect, the patient must sponsor a dance or *candomblé* for, according to the interpretation of the *mãe de santo*, the illness has been caused by an *encosta*. At the *candomblé*, her *filhos da casa* (children of the house, i.e., trained assistants) appear and assist in the treatment. These *filhos*—either men or women, though most often women—are people who have already been treated for an *encosta*, whose *santo* (saint) has been identified, and who have undergone a prescribed period of training during which they have learned songs, rituals and methods of curing. Not all people, therefore, who have been treated by *candomblé* are allowed to work in the cults. The treatment for withdrawing an *encosta* consists of dancing to incessant drumming while the *filhos da casa*, holding the patient by the shoulder, shake him violently. Sometimes these sessions last all night. There are a number of *curadores*—about 25—in the municipality who do not work in *candomblé*. But like the *mães* and *pais de santo*, they prepare medicines which they sell to patients and often *fazem mesas*—that is, hold spiritualist séances. It is in *candomblé*, however, that all these practices have, so to speak, joined hands.

[1] It is difficult to find out how many because these cults are persecuted by both the Church and the police.

Unfortunately, there is no complete ethnography of medieval Portugal, so it is difficult to plot with any degree of accuracy the original contribution of the colonizers. Within recent years, however, the European tradition can be said to be the one most characteristic of Monte Serrat. The manner of dress is of European inspiration. In the city, there are a number of upper-class people who are conscious of high style and in one case a man and his wife sent to Salvador, the capital of the state, for their mourning clothes.

In folklore, food habits, city plan, and in more complex matters such as ideals of status, family organization and official religion, Monte Serrat is oriented more towards Europe than towards either the African or Indian cultures. For the most part, however, people are unaware of the amalgamation which has taken place, and an individual, as such, is not identified with the degree of his participation in one or another of these cultural forms. A person is not an Indian because he does slash-and-burn agriculture or a Negro because he participates in *candomblé*. To the people of the community nothing is particularly aboriginal, African or European. It is Brazilian, *nordestino* or, in most cases, 'the way we do things in Monte Serrat'.

IV. The blending of cultures is paralleled on the physical level by the phenomenon of race mixture. There are very few 'pure' types in Monte Serrat. A 'pure' Negro sometimes appears, as was the case in one of the darker urban families where one of the children, a daughter, 'came out' black. Of the white families, only one is felt by the people of Monte Serrat to be *sem mistura* (without mixture). Yet, even here, there appears to be some question. An older resident of the community, commenting on a member of this family who, after a number of years in the southern part of the country, had returned for a visit, said: 'Before he left, I thought he was of a finer quality' (*qualidade mais fina*). Mulattoes, likewise, can seldom be identified as the result of a simple cross between a Negro and a white. Often, they have a Mongoloid feature or two such as the eye-fold or the flattened malar bones. Another term, *cafuso*, is often used as a label for this intermediate variety, although the word generally refers to a cross between a Negro and an Indian. The only people in the community who are regarded as 'pure' Indian are a man and his wife who have recently moved to Monte Serrat from an *aldeia* (settlement, reservation) and a young woman who works as a servant for her *pai de criação* (father by adoption).

People in Monte Serrat are aware of the extent of race mixture and, on the whole, tend to be rather proud of it. A founder of a nearby community has a favourite story which he tells to illustrate this point. 'What animal', he asks, 'is the strongest you know?'

When the person he is addressing fails to answer, he says: 'The burro! And do you know why? Because the burro is a mixture.' 'Who,' he goes on, 'is the strongest person you know?' When there is no answer to this, he fairly shouts: 'The Brazilian! And why? Because he is a mixture, just like the burro!'[1] At less dramatic moments, this man pointed out that everyone in the community is racially mixed to some degree and that in every family a variety of types is likely to be born. 'In my family, we have Negroes, *mulatos, caboclos*—everything.' The fact of race mixture is officially recognized by the national census. In the most recent census, only three *qualidades* (qualities) were used: *branco, preto* and *pardo*—literally, white, Negro and mixed.[2] In 1940 the classification was *branco, preto, amarelo* and *outros*: white, black, yellow (Indian) and others.

When pressed for specific information, however, people can sometimes discriminate more finely between types. There are, for example, about a half-dozen racial variants which are recognized. A woman of the lower class was familiar with the following categories:

1. *Preto:* very dark skin, with hair in little bunches.
2. *Mulato: caboclo or moreno* with 'good' (i.e., straight) hair.
3. *Cabo verde:* straight hair and 'light-black' skin.
4. *Sarará:* 'ant' colour, with 'bad' hair.
5. *Moreno claro:* 'Dark white' skin, with 'good' hair.
6. *Moreno escuro*: darker than *moreno claro*, but also with 'good' hair.
7. *Branco:* white, with 'good' hair.

An upper-class woman distinguished:

1. *Branco:* well-made mouth, fine lips and nose, 'good' hair.
2. *Preto:* very black, with coarse or curly hair, thick lips and broad nose.
3. *Cabo verde:* black, but with 'good' hair.
4. *Moreno claro:* literally, light brunet.[3]
5. *Moreno alvo:* similar to *moreno claro* but even lighter.[3]
6. *Moreno escuro:* literally, dark brunet.[3]
7. *Moreno côr de canela:* literally, cinnamon coloured.[3]
8. *Amarelo:* 'has no blood'; very pale and with any sort of hair.
9. *Mulato:* not as dark as the *preto* and with 'bad' hair.
10. *Gazo:* very white with blue eyes; 'too white' (albino?).

A lower middle-class woman listed the following:

1. *Branco:* white, with 'good' hair.
2. *Mulato:* black and slightly curled hair; light skin.
3. *Cabo verde:* black skin and straight hair.

[1] The burro, it should be said, is valued above the horse and certainly above the *jegue* (jackass). It is felt that the burro is best adjusted to the ruggedness of the terrain and *pode aguentar mais* (can take more).

[2] Unfortunately, the 1950 census was not available when this paper was being written. It is exceedingly improbable, however, that the ratio of races in this region has changed, since immigration, as already noted, has been slight. See page 89.

[3] The woman, herself, offered no description of the *moreno* types, feeling they were self-evident.

4. *Moreno:* black, 'good' hair and dark skin.
5. *Caboclo:* same as *cabo verde.*

Clearly it is with regard to the mixed type—*os outros* as used in the national census—that the people are unclear as to the physical characteristics. Thus, the lower middle-class woman says that the *mulato* has light skin, the upper-class woman says he has dark skin, and the woman from the lower class says he is a *moreno*, a term which will be explained shortly. The *caboclo*, as a separate type, is mentioned only by the lower middle-class woman, who says he is the same as the *cabo verde*, a type which is distinguished by the other two women as well. The *moreno* is generally splintered into a number of categories, the lower middle-class woman recognizing two while the upper-class woman mentions four. Another fact which becomes evident is that to the people of Monte Serrat, hair is as important as, if not more important than, skin colour when classifying races. To the census interviewers, hair was also an important criterion. 'When it came to a question,' one of them said, 'I always listed a dark person with good hair as a *moreno* and a dark person with bad hair as a Negro.' There have been occasions when the quality of the hair has become a decisive factor in personal relations. A young man was courting a girl whom he happened to meet only at night. Once, when he saw her during the daytime and discovered that she had 'bad' hair, he immediately discontinued their relationship.

Despite the vague manner in which the 'races' are generally identified, people, especially those of the upper class, betray a certain anxiety with regard to their own characteristics. As one adolescent boy expressed it, there is always the fear that someone in the family will 'come out' black. His grandfather, he said, had told him that in slave times it was a common practice to give away those children of white families who were born black, so "Thank the Lord I was not born at that time; though I am not black, I am not a very light colour either'. On one occasion, a group of dark children were observed powdering their faces with ground chalk in order to 'become white'. A man, married to a dark woman, displayed his forearm and said proudly: 'You see, it's white!' Women of whatever colour, are exceedingly proud of giving birth to light-coloured children, for this indicates they have a *barriga limpa*—a clean stomach. A woman who gives birth to a child darker than herself, on the other hand, is said to have a 'dirty stomach'. Men are never held responsible for the *qualidade* of their children and, oddly enough, there are no recognized means by which a woman may 'clean' her stomach. One woman said that people often use purgatives to this end but 'this is *bobagem*' (nonsense). Having a 'clean' or a 'dirty' stomach is a matter of luck or destiny and 'there is nothing that can be done about it'. Non-genetic explanations, however, are often offered to explain the wide range of physical types in the community: it is a matter of climate, several people said.

The word *moreno* (feminine, *morena*), literally brunet, assumes a particular significance in relation to the difficulty—or reluctance—people display in thinking in racial terms, as it refers not so much to race (i.e., ancestry) as to intensity of pigmentation. (It is for this reason that the upper-class woman distinguished four varying qualities of *moreno*). People of whatever racial background may be called *morenos* without suggesting any genetic implication or any of the numerous social qualifications with which each of the races, in their extreme form, is associated. A person of any class may, likewise, be a *moreno*. If he tends towards the darker portion of the spectrum, he would be a *moreno escuro* (dark brunet); if, on the other hand, he tends towards the lighter portion, he would be a *moreno claro* (light brunet). Although it is 'better' to be of the lighter variety, people of both intensities may be found in all classes. The *prefeito* of the municipality is often called a *moreno escuro*, although physically he is of the *caboclo* type, having straight black hair and copper-coloured skin; another of the leading residents of Monte Serrat is also called a *moreno escuro*, though he tends to approach the *mulato*. The judge is a *moreno claro*; one of the schoolteachers is a *morena clara*. One seamstress is a *morena clara* while another is a *morena escura*. This type is often mentioned as the mating ideal. *O moreno de olhos verdes*—the *moreno* with green eyes—is the person most often accorded that gesture of great approval by the people in Monte Serrat: the lobe of the ear grasped by the thumb and forefinger and wiggled.

The word *caboclo*, similarly, has a number of connotations not directly associated with race. Some people associate the *caboclo* with the Indian, or, like the woman of the lower class, equate it with the *moreno*. Others use the word in its more precise sense of a mixture between Indian and white. As mentioned previously, a *caboclo* may be any spirit, an *encosta*, which has entered a person's body and made him ill. What most people in Monte Serrat mean by the word *caboclo*, however, is a native of their region, often a *sertanejo*, and most likely a mixed-blood. '*Nosso caboclo aqui é muito forte*', a man may say, by which he means to indicate, simply, that a person from this part of the country is very strong. The founder of a neighbouring community once described the *caboclo* as 'the strongest person in Brazil: he can go into the *mato* and live for three days on coffee and *raspadura*' (or *rapadura*, a kind of brown sugar prepared as loaves). The people of Monte Serrat are thinking of *caboclo* in this sense when they say that *o caboclo tem muito prestígio em nossa terra* (the caboclo has much prestige in our land). Often, when generalizing about people, they rate the *caboclo* above the Negro and far above the white in terms of vigour. 'He can take more', (*aguenta mais*) or does not fall prey to illness or, most important of all, 'he does not show his age'. He is not always terribly clever, however, and even when he is considered moderately clever, he always ends by betraying himself:

Once a *caboclo* was walking in the *mato* and, becoming tired, he lay down to rest. Two hunters came upon him and, thinking he was dead, decided to carry him to the city. The *caboclo* who had overheard their discussion decided to let them believe what they wished. To get to the city, they had to cross a river which happened to be full. Being unfamiliar with the country-side, they entered the deepest part of the river. The *caboclo*, then, lifted his head and said: 'If you cross over there, it will be easier for you.' The men became so angry with the trick that had been played on them, that they dropped the *caboclo* and let him drown.

White people, by way of contrast, are often felt to embody the nega-tive aspects of the *caboclo*: they are *fracos* (weak), they age rapidly, their blood is bad, and they cannot work hard because they are al-ways sick. They are extremely intelligent—how else account for their success in life? Foreigners, as a group, are sometimes said to be all of *qualidades finas* (of fine quality, i.e., white), intelligent and rich. The Portuguese is probably the one national group which is excluded from this description. There are numerous anecdotes, as there are all over Brazil, to illustrate his supposed stupidity.

Negroes, by and large, are felt to be repugnant. Although oc-casionally someone may say, '*Quem sofre mais é o negro*',[1] (Who suffers most is the *negro*) it is more common to hear an expression such as, '*Éste negro é gente p'ra encostar nêle?*' (Is this *negro* a person you should lean against?), which is what a lower-class woman once told her young daughter. 'All Negroes have ugly mouths', a woman said, or '*Que negro feio danado!*' (What a damned ugly *negro*!) Another woman said that all a Negro was good for was to '*segurar costal de jegue, dar peido em samba, e dar recado a mulher dama*' (take care of a jackass, break wind in a samba, and carry messages to a whore). The Negro is said to be a false friend; if one does not watch him carefully, he will betray the person who is aiding him. Negroes are lazy, another man explained: 'They only work when you force them to; that's why they worked during slave times.' Other people draw more subtle distinctions: 'A Negro is all right,' a public official explained, 'until he gets a 'ring on his finger'—that is, until he is educated—'then he becomes *orgulhoso* (proud) and impossible.'

On the other hand, Negroes are, in certain situations, rated rather highly. '*Quando o negro é sério, é sério mesmo*' (When a *negro* is serious, he is really serious) a man once said. Negresses are often looked upon as being the most passionate lovers. 'We marry *mo-renas*', a man said, 'but Negresses are *mais quentes*' (hotter). They

---

[1] *Negro* is a derogatory term, unlike *preto* which means, simply, black. It is used here with its Brazilian-Portuguese signifiance.

97

are often said to be *mais apertadas* (tighter, with regard to vaginal opening).[1] To sleep with a Negro woman is, in some cases, considered healthful. The story is told of a member of the community who was extremely run down physically and might have been suffering from tuberculosis. He began to live with a Negro woman, by whom he had two children, and in a very short time regained his health. This man is now one of the few homosexuals in Monte Serrat, but he is always pointed out as being *muito forte*, which means that he is both stout and strong. The blood of the Negro is very good, people sometimes say. It is *curativo para o branco* (a curative for the white). Having sexual relations with a Negress is even thought to cure syphilis.

The fact, however, that these preconceived notions of stereotypes are not always operative became apparent in a test which was administered to a representative group of 100 people in the community.[2] A group of eight pictures was used for this experiment; four of the photos were of men and four of women. One pair represented the Negro, another the *caboclo* (Amerindian), a third the mulatto and the fourth the white. Those questioned were then asked to rate the people in the photographs according to a certain number of qualities. The number of votes each person received for each position, with the questions, are summarized in Table II.

It is clear that a certain general pattern exists: by and large the whites are shown preference, while there is a gradual shading off against the Negroes who usually appear in the final position. Thus, the white male is considered to be the most attractive, the wealthiest, the most honest and the most religious. With regard to work, however, he is felt to have the least potentiality. The Negro, in each of these instances, is felt to embody the opposite qualities. The *caboclo* and *mulato* appear regularly in second and third positions, but the ratio varies greatly: the *mulato* was chosen four times for second position and three times for third, while the *caboclo* was selected only once and twice respectively. The situation with regard to the female photographs is fairly similar. The white woman was chosen as the most attractive, the wealthiest and the most honest. The Negress, as one might expect, was felt to be the least attractive, the poorest, the least honest and the least religious. The *cabocla*, for reasons soon to be explained, was selected as the most religious and as both the best and the worst worker. The *mulata* was regularly relegated to second position while the Negress was felt to be third in attractiveness and honesty, the white third in capacity for work and the *mulata* third in

[1] It is interesting to note that in Monte Serrat the expression *fazendo o negro velho* means to have intercourse.

[2] The distribution was as follows: Negro, 2 men, 4 women; white, 22 men, 17 women; mulato, 6 men, 5 women; caboclo 20 men, 24 women.

In some cases, the respondents were indefinite as to their choices; in others they made duplicate selections. The total number of answers, therefore, is sometimes less than 100 and sometimes more.

Table II.

Choice	Male photo				Female photo			
	1st	2nd	3rd	4th	1st	2nd	3rd	4th

1. Which person is most attractive?

Caboclo	11	28	27	21	8	5	25	**50**
Preto	6	9	14	**50**	2	16	**45**	27
Mulato	3	**43**	**35**	5	23	**58**	10	2
Branco	**76**	7	7	5	**61**	22	13	3

2. Which person is the wealthiest?

Caboclo	15	**31**	23	23	34	16	17	28
Preto	21	10	21	**41**	7	12	31	**44**
Mulato	10	29	**34**	18	8	**42**	**36**	9
Branco	**55**	24	13	7	**48**	28	14	9

3. Which person is the best worker?

Caboclo	9	8	**52**	30	**31**	7	14	**43**
Preto	**76**	8	8	9	30	27	21	19
Mulato	11	**70**	14	5	26	**38**	28	7
Branco	5	16	27	**51**	11	28	**40**	23

4. Which person is most honest?

Caboclo	11	27	23	29	31	16	18	30
Preto	17	15	23	**34**	12	18	**30**	**35**
Mulato	21	**28**	**27**	14	16	**49**	20	11
Branco	**37**	24	20	8	**42**	19	28	10

5. Which person is the most religious?

Caboclo	15	20	**33**	24	**60**	10	8	17
Preto	27	14	19	**31**	7	20	28	**38**
Mulato	14	**44**	24	14	14	**40**	**31**	13
Branco	**40**	20	12	17	24	34	23	17

Note: Bold type indicates the leading choice for each position.

wealth and devotion. It should be noted, however, that *not one of the races was totally disqualified for any of the positions.* The number of votes may be small, but each of the types was preferred by a certain number of people.

There are a number of instances, however, where the results appear to diverge from the anticipated scores. The Negro male, for example, was once chosen for the leading position while the white was relegated to the last. In two instances, the *cabocla* superseded the white woman and, in general, found less favour than the *mulata*. Why, in addition, was the white male considered the most religious while the white female was felt to be less devout than the *cabocla*? Fortunately, while the test was being administered, it was possible to judge what led people to react in a certain manner. At the time the test was organized, it was impossible to secure photographs of *caboclos* (i.e., people of basically American-Indian physical type) which could be correlated on all levels with those of the other races. The only available female photograph was of an elderly woman, standing in front of a thatched hut and squinting in what most people considered to be a most unattractive fashion. It was at first considered that the photograph should perhaps be eliminated for this reason. When it became apparent, however, that much information of value could be obtained from its use, it was retained. Looking at the photograph, people would say: '*Que velha feia danada!*' (What a damned ugly old lady!); or: 'Who is the most religious? The old lady, of course.' It was specifically the unattractiveness and the age of the woman, rather than her physical type—which was generally ignored—that either raised or lowered her in the estimation of respondents with regard to the questions asked. Thus, 'as everybody knows', old ladies are ugly, they 'live in church' (unlike young white women) and, because of their responsibilities, might possibly be the hardest workers.

Similar conditions account for the extreme preference shown the mulatto. The photograph of the *caboclo* (male) shows a man with his head turned sideways, thus suggesting to some that he was *desconfiado* (suspicious) and untrustworthy. In the reproduction, again, he appears rather light in colour and not at all of the *moreno* quality generally associated with this type. A number of people, therefore, mistook him for a crafty white man, thus explaining the relatively few votes he received as 'best worker'—scarcely more than the white. The reason the latter was selected as 'most religious', however, is adducible to other factors. A common expression in Monte Serrat is: '*Quem pode ligar à igreja são os brancos*' (Those who can pay attention to the church are the whites). It takes a considerable amount of money to be active in the religious life of the community in terms of special Masses, church decorations, contributions to the brotherhoods and so forth. To most people, full participation in this side of life is consequently impossible. The people most able to *ligar à igreja* are *os bons*—the members of the upper class—who are very often equated with the whites.

Cultural values of an equally subtle nature were invoked in the case of the Negro. Being a good worker is not considered an admirable quality in Monte Serrat—or, for that matter, in Brazil

100

generally. The Puritan notion of associating wealth with the sweat of one's brow is quite foreign to their thinking. The person who works *least* or, at any rate, is engaged in an occupation where he does not have to use his hands, is the one who is accorded most respect.[1] A *roceiro*, for example, would never be regarded as highly as a public official or even an impoverished shopkeeper. Work, it is often said, is for Negroes and burros (donkeys). The selection of the Negro as 'best worker', therefore, is perfectly reasonable from the point of view of the local culture. If the question were re-phrased as: 'Whom do you consider the worst worker?' the white, as in all other respects, would be found in the leading position.

The physical type of a person alone, however, is not enough to account for the complex reactions of the people, for, as throughout Brazil, race is defined as much by social as by phycisal facts. A person, regardless of his colour, may be referred to as a *preto*; a mother may criticize her young daughter for acting boisterously in the *praça* by saying she is carrying on like a *negrinha*—that is, like a low-class person. The class a person is associated with as well as personal feelings may either raise or lower him in the eyes of his neighbours. This became specially clear when statistics were being gathered on the standards of living in the community. Men who had worked on the national census were employed to do this work and, among the things they were asked to note was the race of the people they interviewed. Explanations were given them of what was meant by race in terms of those traits used by physical anthropologists: a Negro, for example, was described as having a very dark skin, a broad nose, everted lips and tightly curled or even woolly hair. Despite the careful briefing, there were a number of cases where the census takers' classifications differed from that which an anthropologist would make. People of high status who might have been identified as *caboclo* or even mulatto were sometimes listed as white and, conversely, people of low status who might have been classified as white were sometimes described as being darker in colour. The expression, 'money lightens the skin', which is familiar to the people of Monte Serrat though seldom used, is thus as true of this community as of other parts of Brazil.

To determine the extent to which race and class are associated in Monte Serrat, a list was drawn up of 20 well-known individuals in the community, belonging to the various classes as well as the several racial groups. Sixty-three people, also representative of the community, were then asked to classify the people on the list.[2] To avoid confusion, they were allowed to use only four racial categories and three classes, namely, white, Negro, mulatto and *caboclo*[3] for the

---

[1] In Monte Serrat, men of the upper class often allow the nail of their little finger to grow long.
[2] The distribution of respondents was as follows: Class I, 14; Class II, 14; Class III, 35.
[3] Meaning a basically Amerindian type.

TABLE III.[1]

Group	Race and class according to informants						
	I	II	III	Preto	Branco	Mulatto	Caboclo

People the writer considered Class I and white

Group	I	II	III	Preto	Branco	Mulatto	Caboclo
Fazendeiro	57	4	1	1	53	6	2
Fazendeiro	42	5	0	1	56	3	0
Teacher	56	6	0	1	35	19	6
The Writer	59	2	0	0	59	1	1
Functionary	59	3	0	0	57	2	0
Functionary	36	26	0	1	56	6	0

People the writer considered Class II and white

Group	I	II	III	Preto	Branco	Mulatto	Caboclo
Shoemaker	7	40	13	0	50	9	4

People the writer considered Class III and white

Group	I	II	III	Preto	Branco	Mulatto	Caboclo
Prostitute	2	5	50	0	43	6	4
Shoemaker	5	23	30	0	53	4	2

People the writer considered Class I and mulatto

Group	I	II	III	Preto	Branco	Mulatto	Caboclo
Comerciante	34	22	9	5	8	28	16

People the writer considered Class II and mulatto

Group	I	II	III	Preto	Branco	Mulatto	Caboclo
Comerciante	3	41	17	11	7	34	11
Housewife	5	33	20	3	28	20	7
Official	11	26	11	4	5	36	15

People the writer considered Class III and mulatto

Group	I	II	III	Preto	Branco	Mulatto	Caboclo
Candy-maker	2	19	38	16	0	27	7

People the writer considered Class I and *caboclo*

Group	I	II	III	Preto	Branco	Mulatto	Caboclo
Comerciante	57	5	0	2	9	24	27

People the writer considered Class II and *caboclo*

Group	I	II	III	Preto	Branco	Mulatto	Caboclo
Announcer	8	32	23	2	2	24	35
Hotel-keeper	5	33	20	3	28	20	7

People the writer considered Class III and *caboclo*

Group	I	II	III	Preto	Branco	Mulatto	Caboclo
Seamstress	1	29	28	2	1	8	51
Mason	0	26	33	3	2	23	31

[1] Only one Negro was used on the list. The writer classified her as Class III. Of the respondents, 52 felt she was Class III, five listed her as Class II and two people as Class I. With respect to race, 60 people felt she was Negro, two said she was *mulata* and one that she was a *cabocla*.

races and one, two and three for the classes. In Table III, the names have been deleted and the occupations of the persons have been substituted. They are divided into the racial and social groups where the writer, who happens to be one of the people on the list, would place them.

Even a cursory glance at Table III indicates that, roughly speaking, there is a high correlation between light skin colour and membership of the upper class. But it is not a perfect correlation—there are enough exceptions to the general rule to indicate that variables, aside from these two, are operating. It is with these variables that we are now concerned. Among the people assigned to the category 'Class I', one person, an official, was rated as upper class by 36 people while the sizeable number of 26 people considered him to be middle-class. The man himself, who was one of the people who responded to the questionnaire, was rather indeterminate as to his exact status. 'There is no upper class in Monte Serrat,' he pointed out. At first he nominated himself for middle class; it was only later, upon the insistence of his family, that he asked to be changed to upper class. Compared to some others in the community, this man is not rich. Although a public official, he is now retired.[1] He has begun to participate in the sisal boom, but only on a limited scale. In politics, he is associated with the minority party rather than with the party in power. Even more important, he is not a *filho daqui*—a son of Monte Serrat—and, although his family has been living in the municipality for a considerable time, they have no 'historical depth' so far as the people are concerned. The doubtfulness of his class status is a result of a combination of these circumstances.

The teacher was considered Class I by 59 people, while only two people felt she was Class II. However, in the racial aspect of the test there is a far greater discrepancy. Of a total of 61 people, 35 considered her white, 19 felt she was a *mulata* and six others considered her a *cabocla*, giving a total of 25 for the intermediate group, while one person said she was a Negress. The explanation most often given for this wide range in racial aperception was that 'she couldn't be white because there were *pretos* in her family'. Her father, it was pointed out, was quite dark; her brother is also dark and another brother 'came out' almost *preto*. Consequently she is not 'pure'. Family, therefore, in its genetic sense, becomes important as a race criterion. It was used in a number of other instances: the two *fazendeiros* were considered mulatto by a few people because they, likewise, had *pretos* in their family. In numerous instances people who were interviewed said that they could not indicate the *qualidade* of some of the people on the list because they 'did not know their family' (*não conheço a família dêle*). This was particularly the case

---

[1] Retired public officials continue to receive their salary and are often referred to by their titles.

with regard to the writer, although it occurred sufficiently often with people who were actual residents of the community.

In other instances, different criteria were invoked. A woman defined as Class II *mulata* by the writer was felt to be Class II by 33 people, Class I by five and Class III by 20. Only 20 people, however, felt she was a *mulata*; 28 people said she was white, seven said she was *cabocla*, and three that she was a Negress. It is significant that both the woman and her husband, who responded to the questionnaire, did not vote with the majority of the people: both felt she was a *mulata* of Class III. The children of this union, like the mother, are often considered white by the people of Monte Serrat, although one is definitely a *cabocla*, having both the facial features associated with this group as well as the long, black hair which she proudly displays. The reason for the apparent discrepancies, suggested by the writer, is that the husband and father of this family is white. His wife and children, by proximity, have been lightened. This tendency to lighten people is apparent in a number of other cases. It was certainly of importance in connexion with both the upper-class mulatto and the upper-class *caboclo*, both of whom were felt to be white by a number of people. In the main, however, this seems to operate on a class level. People tend to lighten people of their own class while they appear more critical of those either above or below them. 'Don't say you are a *preta*,' a woman of the lower class said to another who was answering the questionnaire, 'you are always trying to lower yourself.'

A further criterion which operated in numerous cases was that of personal association. A man of Class I was calles *preto* by a woman, although most people considered him white, because of a bitter argument she had recently had with him. The reason that some people felt the writer was either a *mulato* or *caboclo* was because he had 'bad' hair. In at least three cases, the respondents seemed undecided as to which racial category a person belonged. An upper-class *comerciante* was called *mulato* by 24 people and *caboclo* by 27; the announcer was felt to be *caboclo* by 35 people and *mulato* by 24; and the votes for the hotel-keeper were mainly divided between *mulato* and *branco*. The chief reason for this has already been suggested: the people do not distinguish easily the physical characters of the mixed group. A *moreno* may be considered either a *caboclo* or a *mulato*. It is more difficult to determine the reasons for dividing the votes for the hotel-keeper between the mulatto and the *white*. Actually, the man is rather dark; his hair is not 'bad'. It is possible that his importance in both the political and economic life of the community affected the distribution of his votes.

The results of this test were, in most respects, consistent with another experiment which was conducted in Monte Serrat. People were asked to grade the photographs, which had been used earlier to

determine the racial stereotypes, in terms of social classification.[1]
Five questions were asked, and the distribution of the affirmative
answers is given in Table IV. The anticipated pattern once again
appears. In every instance, the white male and female were chosen
for the leading positions, while the Negroes, by and large, were felt
to be the least desirable associates. In answer to questions 3, 4 and 5,
however, the *caboclo* female found less favour than her Negro counterpart. The votes for the intermediate groups were equally divided

TABLE IV.[2]

Questions	Caboclo		Preto		Mulato		Branco	
	M.	*F.*	*M.*	*F.*	*M.*	*F.*	*M.*	*F.*
1. Would you accept this person as a neighbour?	48	37	*20*	*30*	34	59	**81**	**79**
2. Would you accept this person as a friend?	52	44	*21*	*33*	38	59	**84**	**77**
3. Would you invite this person to dinner?	51	*38*	*31*	43	45	62	**75**	**77**
4. Would you allow your son (daughter) to dance with this person?	53	*57*	*35*	62	53	76	**77**	**88**
5. Would you accept this person as a brother-in-law (sister-in-law)?	43	*41*	23	43	37	60	**64**	**76**

[2] The highest score for each question appears in bold type, the lowest in italics. For a more detailed
breakdown of this data see Appendix II.

in the sense that the *mulato* female was in each case preferred to the
caboclo female, while the *caboclo* male was generally preferred to
the *mulato* male. As in the case of the stereotypes, it was the unattractiveness and the age of the *caboclo* woman which most often
compelled people to discount her other qualities, while it was the

[1] The distribution in this case was done according to class and colour:

	Men-class			Women-class		
	I	*II*	*III*	*I*	*II*	*III*
Negro	0	0	2	0	0	4
White	7	13	2	7	5	5
Mulatto	1	1	4	0	1	4
Caboclo	1	4	15	1	6	17
TOTAL	9	18	23	8	12	30

Once again, some of the respondents were indefinite as to their selection. The totals, therefore, do not
always come to a fixed number.

nature of the photograph which made some people feel that the *caboclo* male was a less personable white man. There is another tendency which is equally important. The votes for each of the racial groups, except in certain cases which will be considered subsequently, fall within a very definite range. Thus, the *caboclo* male received 48 votes as a neighbour, 52 a as friend, 51 a as dinner companion, 53 as a dancing partner, and 43 as a prospective brother-in-law. The Negro male, similarly, received 20 votes as a neighbour, 21 as a friend, 31 for dinner, 35 as a dancing partner and 23 as a brother-in-law. It may be concluded, therefore, that, aside from variables, each of the races is accorded a definite level of tolerance.

Space does not permit a complete analysis of the responses according to race, sex and class. By referring to the more detailed analysis in Appendix II, however, it can be seen that there is a considerable range. Although the white male was generally chosen for the first position by all the races, the Negroes showed a slight preference for the mulatto in questions 1 and 4 (Would you accept this man as your neighbour? Would you allow your daughter to dance with this man?) and in answer to the third question (Would you invite this man to dinner?) they divided their votes equally between the mulatto and the white. There is even more variation with regard to the second and third positions. Although the *caboclo* (male) was in most instances preferred to the mulatto and the *preto*, the Negroes selected the white male as their second most desirable neighbour while the mulattoes divided their votes equally between the *caboclo* and mulatto. In answer to the second question (Would you accept this man as your friend?), the Negroes gave three votes each to the *preto* and mulatto while, according to the 'sexual' breakdown, the women gave 22 votes each to the *caboclo* and mulatto. As a dinner guest, the Negroes (possibly because of the tie for first position between the mulatto and the white) selected the *preto* while, judged by the social grouping, the people of Class III chose the mulatto above the *caboclo* by one vote. As a dancing partner for their daughter, there is considerable variation: for second position, the Negroes selected the white, the whites and mulattoes chose the mulatto, and the *caboclos* preferred their own race; respondents from Class I chose the *caboclo* while the other two groups selected the mulatto—while with regard to sex, men and women chose, respectively, the *caboclo* and mulatto. As second choice for brother-in-law, the Negroes and mulattoes showed a slight preference for their own races.

Reactions to the female photographs were, in most respects, much the same as for the males (see Appendix III). Thus, the white woman was generally selected as most desirable except that in almost every case she shared her position with one or more of the other types. In answer to the first question (Would you accept this woman as your neighbour?) for example, the Negroes cast an equal number of votes for the *mulata*, as they did in response to the second question (Would you accept this woman as your friend?). For the third and fourth questions (Would you invite this woman to dinner? Would you allow your son to dance with her?) they divided their votes equally among the *preta*, *mulata* and *branca*. While the Negress was generally found to be least desirable—fourth position—as a neighbour and as a friend, it was the *cabocla* who in most cases was not wanted as a dinner guest, a dancing partner for their son or a sister-in-law. The rejection of the *cabocla* (female), on the other hand, is not as great as that of the Negro male. In the intermediate positions there is again considerable range according to class, sex and colour. On the average, however, the *mulata* gained second place while for third the votes were divided fairly regularly between the Negress and the *cabocla*. It is evident, therefore, that in each situation numerous factors must be considered when evaluating the responses.

The questions must be evaluated also from the point of view of the local culture. Hospitality, for example, is an almost universal custom in Monte Serrat. In the rural area, any stranger who appears might be given the freedom of the house, *('a casa é sua'*, people say— the house is yours) as well as lodging and food; while a person might not prefer to have a certain individual as a neighbour or a brother-in-law, it is less likely that he would be refused these amenities. It was for this reason that the *caboclo* (male) received more votes as a dinner guest than as a neighbour or as a mate for one's sister. The Negro, similarly, achieved a higher score with regard to dinner than as a neighbour, a friend or a brother-in-law. Dancing, also, cannot be considered on the same level as most of the other questions. For most people, this is one of the most relished diversions. 'I could live in *festas*', a young man of the lower class once said. A woman, while relating her biography, said: 'When I was young, all I wanted to do was dance.' Many people, therefore, when asked if their son or daughter could dance with any of the people in the photographs said: 'Of course; it will do no harm.' (*Não faz mal*). It was more usual, however, for a man or woman to say that it was acceptable for their *son* to dance with any of these people, while their *daughter*— well, that was another question.

With these qualifications, however, the picture presented by the statistics may be considered an accurate gauge of the way people feel about the races with which they live. When the types are clearly defined as either black or white, the responses are fairly definite. With the middle group, however, the large mass of the population which is most often called *moreno* rather than either *caboclo* or *mulato*, one does not find the same consistency. It is true that *caboclos* or *mulatos* never reach the position of the whites; on the other hand, under ordinary circumstances, they do not descend to

107

that of the Negroes. They remain truly intermediate. When they rise to a position above their group or, as in the case of the *cabocla* (woman) fall beneath it, one must seek other factors to determine the cause.

V. In many respects, Monte Serrat is in a transitional phase. The introduction of a new cash crop which has proved successful has caused profound changes in several aspects of the society. The traditional respect for the old families is breaking down in the face of circumstances which make it possible for a person to 'buy' himself important connexions. The ideal of personal independence, which formerly depended upon the goodwill of one's extended family and the numerous personal relationships that were the result of the close co-operation demanded by a close-to-subsistence economy, is now made possible by hiring oneself out for a time with the hope that eventually one may accumulate enough capital to become a successful *comerciante* oneself. This does not mean to say that the system has completely accommodated itself to the new situation. The tensions of which one becomes aware, as well as the irresolution people often display in social situations that were at one time as carefully patterned as a mosaic, are directly associated with the rapidity with which the entire society is changing. This is more marked, or course, in the city of Monte Serrat than in the rural areas, where it is still common for a person to ask a blessing of an individual of superior status, whether or not that person is an actual or ritual relative or a complete stranger. Nevertheless, the speed with which the most important aspects of the society are becoming reconciled to the social facts is remarkable.

It is, therefore, understandable that race, as one of the features of class, should likewise be adjusting itself to the same set of circumstances. So far, it has not become the only focus of status. During the last *prefeitural* election, for example, there was no mention of the fact that one of the contenders—the man who was finally selected—was a *moreno escuro* of the *caboclo* type, while the opposition candidate was white. Only much later did one of the leading residents comment upon this. It would have been better, he said, if the other man had been elected since he was of a '*qualidade mais fina*'. Otherwise, he commented wryly, there was nothing to recommend either of them since they were both almost illiterate and had had no experience in politics. It is likewise rare for family conflicts to be solely in terms of race. Occasionally, it is true, one is told that when a white girl falls in love with a Negro it is because the latter has made a *feitiço* for her, (practised black magic); or that it is unwise for a Negro to marry a white person because, should something go wrong

108

with the marriage, the fact of his race would be held accountable. It is much more common for people to recall instances of inter-racial marriage which were successful. Several people were familiar with the case of a Negro *mestre de música* (music teacher) who became enamoured of a white girl. The girl's parents were outraged and tried to discourage the affair. The girl, however, arranged to meet her lover secretly. The method by which this was done was fantastically ingenious. The people in Monte Serrat are horribly afraid of the *lobishomem*, the werewolf character which plays an important role in their folklore. It is a tradition that the *lobishomem* appears, generally, on all the Fridays of Lent. On these days, therefore, the man used to roll down the cobbled streets in a barrel. The people, thinking it was a werewolf, would shut themselves in their houses. Then, once the streets were deserted, the girl was able to meet her lover with complete certainty that they would not be observed. Eventually, this couple married and are said to be living in the capital where they are extremely happy.

Aside from its piquant aspects, this case illustrates numerous attitudes which are significant in Monte Serrat. First of all, it is another indication of the 'cleverness' of the Negro. Secondly, it was, as people say; '*As pessoas de primeira qualidade que fizeram questão* (People of the first quality who objected). It would be exceptional for a really dark person to interfere with the marriage of his son, let us say, to a lighter person. It would be equally rare, however, for a white father to accept such a situation with equanimity. 'In the olden days,' an informant explained, 'people of good families would only let their children marry *entre parentes* (among relatives). That was how they kept their families clean.'[1] In recent times, however, once a mixed marriage seems inevitable, it is accepted with a sort of philosophical resignation, although it may continue to cause comment in the community.[2] Thirdly, in order for this particular marriage to find social acceptance, it was necessary for the couple to leave Monte Serrat and settle in another city. Although there are a few examples of people who remain to face relative ostracism, the social tension in these circumstances is commonly resolved by having

[1] The preferred marriage in Monte Serrat is still of this order. In 1950, about 30 per cent of the marriages were *entre parentes*.

[2] It is possible that the highly developed concept of romantic love assumes added significance with regard to this aspect of the society. There are a number of instances where a person died *apaixonada* (heart-broken, overwhelmed with love) because he—or, more generally, she—was unable to marry the person of his choice. One of the more striking examples concerns the family which may be considered to be the aristocrats of Monte Serrat. The eldest daughter of this family had fallen in love with a chauffeur. He was not of a *qualidade inferior*, but he lacked those refinements demanded by the parents of a prospective mate for their daughter: he was neither college-educated nor did he have a 'family'. When the girl was forced to abandon her lover, she suffered a nervous collapse and eventually died. The other daughters of this family are now engaged to people of either 'inferior quality' or of low social status; and people feel that the reason their parents have not seriously interfered is because of their experience with the first child. The few cases of suicide which people remember are, likewise, related to misfortunes in love.

the people remove themselves physically from the people they might embarrass.[1]

It is precisely because of such difficulties that instances in which people of darker colours have risen in status and gained social approval become significant. The most outstanding example in recent years is the *prefeito* of Monte Serrat. In physical type, as mentioned elsewhere, he is a *caboclo*. His family is generally looked upon as lacking in those virtues which are considered essential to a person of his status: they are not educated, they work mainly as subsistence farmers, they are almost always dark in colour, and they are noted for their violent moods. '*A raça ruim*' is how they are usually described. At one time, people say, it would have been impossible for a person with such a background to become important in the community. Within the past few years, however, this man has become the leading *comerciante* in Monte Serrat. He has numerous warehouses throughout the municipality where he stores produce, mainly sisal, which he buys at the fairs and a fleet of trucks which he sends regularly to the larger cities with the merchandise he has accumulated during the week. His position, people feel, is due entirely to his success as an entrepreneur.

Another example is that of a mulatto government official whose mother was a slave. For many years, he told people that he was going to marry into one of the important families in Monte Serrat. He was considered *orgulhoso* (proud or uppity) and many people were amused by his aspirations. The girl he wanted to court was furious at the attention he paid her and, apparently, was subjected to an inordinate amount of ridicule; but eventually, when she saw that unless she married the mulatto she would remain an old maid, she accepted him. In the beginning, her family was offended and many people in Monte Serrat expected that the marriage would not last. It soon became obvious, however, that the union was going to be successful and the man has since become important in both the public and commercial life of the community.

A third interesting case concerns a young woman, a Negress, who wished to be elected queen of Monte Serrat. As a means of raising money for the Christmas of the Poor, the upper-class people of the community organized a *festa*. As part of the activities, they planned to elect a queen who, in turn, would select a young man to reign as king. An individual was able to purchase as many votes as he wished or could afford. Partly as a joke, but partly because her fiancé wanted her to be elected, people began to purchase votes for the young woman whom I shall call Naga. A few days before the scheduled festival, word was spread through the community that Naga had reached second place and it was likely that, even if not

---

[1] This is likewise the case with the prostitutes, many of whom have continued to visit their families in the *caatingas* and to entertain them as guests in their own houses, but who no longer live with them.

110

elected queen, she might be chosen a princess. People at once became incensed at the possibility. It is significant that people of her own class as well as *os bons* reacted in similar fashion. A lower-class woman said: 'Who does that Negress think she is? Why, it would be scandalous to have a Negro queen in Monte Serrat!' Another person of the lower class said, when asked if he did not think that Naga was attractive: 'What! A Negress attractive! That's impossible!' The situation was further aggravated by Naga's fiancé who mocked an upper-class girl, who also hoped to be elected, by telling her that Naga would doubtless get more votes. The problem was resolved in autocratic but characteristic fashion: Naga was outlawed. The day before the final votes were cast, the officials of the *festa* announced over the loudspeaker that the money which had been collected in her name would be given to her as a gift, but that she was no longer one of the candidates. Immediately afterwards no one spoke of what had happened, aside from Naga's friends who continued to tantalize her about her 'uppity notions'. Naga herself, however, was considerably affected. She became quite ill as a result of the incident.

These three cases—the *prefeito*, the mulatto, and the aspiring beauty queen—reveal a number of things about the racial situation in Monte Serrat. First of all, race alone is not a determining factor in social status. If a person has acquired prestige in a number of different ways—through education, through the acquisition of economic importance, or through marrying upward in the social scale, even though of 'inferior quality' he or she may be admitted into the upper class. It is only when a person lacks all other attributes associated with high status that race alone may be decisive, as in the case of Naga. As an illustration of this point, a similar *festa*, held in the neighbouring community of Mato Branco, may be used. Mato Branco is an economic and political rival of Monte Serrat. Shortly after the latter community held its *Festa da Rainha* (Festival of the Queen), the upper class in Mato Branco decided that they would sponsor a similar *festa* in their community. One of the candidates for the position of queen was a '*morena* with bad hair' and, thus, a *mulata*. When the final voting was announced, this young lady had achieved second place and was named one of the princesses of the *festa*. She was chosen because her *parentes* were important in the commercial and social life of the community. She was, unlike Naga, upper-class.

It is impossible to predict with any degree of certainty what form the relations among the races in Monte Serrat will take in the near future. There are indications, for example, that class conflict may become defined more sharply in racial terms. One of the leading *comerciantes* in Monte Serrat once said, during an argument: 'It is right that Negroes should work for whites!' His pronouncement was all the more remarkable as he himself is an extremely dark *caboclo*, of the same *qualidade* as the woman he was reprimanding. In other cities of the north-east, the cleavage between the races has become even more marked. In Joazeiro do Norte, there are a number of clubs to which Negroes are not admitted *because* they are Negroes. As yet, this has not occurred in Monte Serrat. Dark people may mingle with light ones if allowed to by their social position. In the United States people who are defined as Negro may try to improve their status by 'passing for white'; in Monte Serrat they may seek an opportunity to 'pass for upper-class'. As long as mechanisms are provided to make such a transition possible and as long as people are given an opportunity—economically and otherwise—to make use of these mechanisms, it is unlikely that the existing antagonisms among the races will become a serious social problem in Monte Serrat.

APPENDIX I.
Government Officials[1]

Office	Race	Class
MUNICIPAL		
Prefeito	Caboclo	Upper
Secretary	White	Upper
Treasurer	White	Upper
Comptroller	White	Upper-middle
Stenographer	White	Upper-middle
Assistant Stenographer . . .	Mulatto	Lower-middle
General Assistant	White	Upper
Porter	White	Lower
STATE		
Collector	White	Upper-middle
Secretary	White	Upper
Guard	White	Lower-middle
Judge	White	Upper
District Attorney	White	Upper
Police Chief	Mulatto	Upper
School Inspector	Caboclo	Upper
Registrar	Caboclo	Upper-middle
Notary	White	Upper-middle
FEDERAL		
Collector	White	Upper
Secretary	White	Upper
Mail Clerk	White	Upper
Statistics Agent	White	Upper-middle

[1] Teachers, soldiers and a few others are not included.

112

Shopkeepers[1]

Type	Race	Class
LARGE		
Grocer	White	Upper-middle
Grocer	Mulatto	Upper
Grocer	Caboclo	Upper-middle
Grocer	Caboclo	Upper-middle
Grocer	Caboclo	Upper-middle
Drygoods	Caboclo	Upper
Drygoods	Caboclo	Upper-middle
Drygoods	White	Upper
Drygoods	White	Upper-middle
SMALL		
Drygoods	Caboclo	Lower-middle
General	Caboclo	Lower-middle
General	White	ʾInner
General	Caboclo	L ·middle
General	White	Lo middle
General	Caboclo	Lower-middle
General	Caboclo	Lower-middle
General	Caboclo	Lower-middle
General	White	Lower-middle
General	Caboclo	Lower-middle
General	Caboclo	Lower-middle

[1] A number of shops open only at weekends are not included.

BIBLIOGRAPHY

1. James (1948), p. 658.
2. James (1946), p. 51. *See also* Marchant (1942), p. 28 ff.
3. James (1946), p. 53.
4. *Ibid.*, p. 53.

APPENDIX II. Social Distance Tests

(a) Male Photographs

	Distribution of Respondents								
	Race				Class			Sex	
	N.	*W.*	*M.*	*C.*	*I*	*II*	*III*	*M.*	*F.*
	6	39	11	44	17	30	53	50	50

1. Would you accept this man as a neighbour?

Caboclo	2	18	4	24	7	14	27	26	22
Preto	2	5	2	11	2	6	12	9	11
Mulato	5	10	4	15	3	8	23	17	17
Branco	4	32	7	38	14	25	42	36	45

2. Would you accept this man as a friend?

Caboclo	2	18	7	25	9	16	27	30	22
Preto	3	4	3	11	0	5	16	9	12
Mulato	3	9	5	21	1	12	25	16	22
Branco	5	30	10	39	15	24	45	38	46

3. Would you invite this man to dinner?

Caboclo	3	17	5	26	7	14	30	27	24
Preto	4	7	2	18	3	6	22	16	15
Mulato	5	14	5	21	4	10	31	21	24
Branco	5	28	6	36	13	20	42	35	40

4. Would you let your daughter dance with him?

Caboclo	3	15	7	28	5	4	34	26	27
Preto	3	9	4	19	2	9	24	15	20
Mulato	5	16	8	24	2	15	36	25	28
Branco	4	29	9	35	11	21	45	34	43

5. Would you accept him as a brother-in-law?

Caboclo	3	12	8	20	3	11	29	19	24
Preto	4	6	5	8	1	6	16	12	11
Mulato	6	9	6	16	1	9	27	17	20
Branco	6	17	8	33	8	15	41	33	31

(b) Female Photographs

	Distribution of Respondents								
	Race				Class			Sexe	
	N.	*W.*	*M.*	*C.*	*I*	*II*	*III*	*M.*	*F.*
	6	39	11	44	17·	30	53	50	50

1. Would you accept this woman as a neighbour?

Cabocla	5	11	4	17	5	10	22	20	17
Preta	4	7	3	16	1	7	22	13	17
Mulata	6	22	6	25	4	20	35	28	31
Branca	6	29	8	36	7	27	45	40	39

2. Would you accept this woman as a friend?

Cabocla	5	14	5	20	5	11	28	22	22
Preta	5	12	5	11	3	10	20	12	21
Mulata	6	23	7	23	9	16	34	25	34
Branca	6	27	9	35	11	20	46	36	41

3. Would you invite this woman to dinner?

Cabocla	3	11	5	19	4	10	24	23	15
Preta	6	12	5	20	5	7	31	21	22
Mulata	6	22	7	27	6	17	39	32	30
Branca	6	27	9	35	12	18	47	38	39

4. Would you allow your son to dance with her?

Cabocla	5	20	7	25	9	14	34	30	27
Preta	6	21	7	28	9	15	38	30	32
Mulata	6	28	11	31	13	21	42	38	38
Branca	6	31	11	40	15	24	49	42	46

5. Would you accept her as a sister-in-law?

Cabocla	4	9	5	23	2	11	28	20	21
Preta	4	12	6	21	1	10	32	19	24
Mulata	5	17	8	30	3	18	39	28	32
Branca	6	26	10	34	11	19	46	35	41

RACE
RELATIONS
IN AN AMAZON
COMMUNITY[1]

by
CHARLES WAGLEY

I. The great Amazon Valley is one of the most distinctive regions of Brazil. The striking tropical environment, the natural system of communications afforded by the Amazon River and its tributaries, the physical contribution of the' American Indian to the formation of the present population, the persistence of aboriginal traits, and the characteristic extractive industries which are the basis of its economic life are all factors which have combined to produce a distinctive regional variety of Brazilian national culture.

Like other aspects of this Amazon regional culture, inter-racial relations differ somewhat from those encountered in other parts of Brazil. In the Amazon all three racial stocks—the European Caucasoid, the African Negro, and the American Indian—which have entered into the formation of the modern Brazilian population are present. But they are present in different proportions than elsewhere in Brazil. Race mixture has occurred in the Amazon with approximately the same—if not greater—frequency as it has throughout Brazil; but it has taken place under different historical and social circumstances. Common Brazilian attitudes, modes of behaviour, and concepts regarding each racial group are conditioned by the regional society and culture of which they are a part. The Amazon Valley is an integral part of Brazil, and yet it stands out as a characteristic cultural area of this enormous nation.

The relations between the 'racial groups' which make up the present population of the Brazilian Amazon can only be understood within the context of this regional society and culture, and in terms of the trends of regional history. As elsewhere in Brazil, the Portuguese colonist came to the Amazon seeking a fortune. But in the Amazon Valley the terrain did not lend itself to the establishment of a plantation system producing sugar for the world, as it did along the north-east coast. Nor was gold discovered, as in the central plateau region of Minas Gerais and southern Bahia in the eighteenth century. The best the colonist could do in the Amazon Valley was to extract the so-called *drogas do sertão*, products of the tropical forest such as hardwoods, cinnamon, *urucú* and cocoa, for sale in Europe. It was not a very lucrative trade and the colonists were not able to afford to buy African slaves, as were the plantation owners of the north-east coast and the mine owners of the central mountain region.

[1] The field work on which this report is based was carried out under the auspices of Unesco as a preliminary survey for the International Institute of the Hylean Amazon. The research was also sponsored by the Council for Research in the Social Sciences of Columbia University. I wish to thank Clara Galvão, Eduardo Galvão, and Cecilia Roxo Wagley, who also participated in the field research, for making their field notes available to me.

Relatively few Europeans were therefore attracted to this part of Brazil and the number of Negro slaves in the region was insignificant.

Only during the period between about 1880 and 1912, when the Amazon Valley had a world monopoly of forest rubber, was the area a relatively prosperous part of Brazil; after 1912, when competition from the Eastern plantations caused the collapse of the high price for wild rubber, the Amazon again became an isolated and depressed region. The isolation of the Amazon region from the rest of the country has been an important factor in the persistence of numerous traditional culture patterns in the rural areas of the Valley.

The small number of Portuguese colonists who came to live in the Valley after 1616, when Belém was founded near the mouth of the river, were forced to depend upon the rather sparse Indian population to work for them. They needed the Indians as collectors of forest products, as agriculturalists to grow food for them, and in fact for all types of manual labour. They soon resorted to slavery to secure Indian labour. Numerous raids penetrated into the interior, returning with Indian slaves but leaving behind numerous corpses of Indian men, women, and children. The aboriginal population along the mainstream and along the lower tributaries of the Valley would certainly soon have been liquidated if it had not been for the missionaries who arrived in the Amazon with the first Portuguese military expedition. In the seventeenth century religious orders, especially the Jesuits, were competing with the colonist for the Indian. The colonist needed and wanted Indian slaves, while the missionary wanted to protect the Indians from the colonist in order to make Christians of them.

The missionaries established *aldeiamentos*—or mission stations— at strategic points along the Amazon river system, into which they attracted large numbers of Indians from various tribal groups. Under the paternalistic régime of the Jesuits and other missionary orders, these Indians were taught Christian ritual and ideology, new handicrafts and European customs. The colonists, however, continued their slave-raiding, even attacking mission stations. Although edicts were issued from time to time prohibiting slavery, the colonists found numerous legal loopholes which allowed them to go on taking slaves. They prevailed upon the Crown to allow them to make slaves of 'prisoners of just wars' and of Indians 'ransomed from the cord' (i.e., snatched from the hands of cannibals). 'Just wars' and 'cannibalism' increased vertiginously, and Indian slavery continued. In the middle of the eighteenth century, however, when the Jesuits were expelled from Brazil, the control of the Indians passed into civil hands, and the mission stations were transformed into civil towns and villages. Indian slavery was again outlawed, but Indians were subjected to compulsory labour for the colonists, for which by law they were supposed to be paid. This system soon disintegrated

117

into a form of peonage and of debt servitude, which persisted in the Amazon until the present century, and outright slavery was reported in isolated areas until late in the nineteenth century.

The result of both the protective activities of the missionaries and the 'slave raiding' of the colonist was the assimilation and acculturation of the Amazon Indian. It is estimated that the Amazon Valley never contained more than 500,000 aboriginal people, and by 1850 the majority of these had been brought into the orbit of Luso-Brazilian life. Under the reforms promulgated by the famous Portuguese Prime Minister, the Marquess of Pombal, during the second half of the eighteenth century, miscegenation between the Europeans and Indians, which had begun early in the seventeenth century, increased considerably. Portuguese male colonists were offered special inducements—in the form of land grants, free tools, tax exemptions, and even political posts—to marry native women. By 1852, it was estimated that 52 per cent of the population of the Valley were Indians, 26 per cent *mamelucos* (Indian-European mixtures), and the rest Europeans and their few Negro slaves. [1][1]

Today, only some 30,000 to 40,000 tribal Indians remain in the Amazon Valley—an insignificant part of the 1,500,000 people who inhabit the region. But the genetic influence of the American Indian in the modern Amazon population is very apparent. According to the 1940 census, more than 50 per cent of the people of the Amazonian states of Brazil were classed as *pardo*, or brown; 40 per cent as *branco*, or white, and the remainder as *preto*, or Negro. Although the category of *pardo*, as used in Brazil, includes various combinations of Caucasoid, Amerind, and Negro mixtures, it is the impression of most observers that a large proportion of these *pardos*—and many people classed as 'white' as well—have American Indian ancestors. It would be safe to estimate that at least 50 per cent of the people of the Amazon are at least partly of Indian descent.

As early as the 1850's these Amazon 'Indians' and *mamelucos* were, socially and culturally, Brazilian peasants, despite their physical characteristics and the language which most of the rural population spoke at that time. Since the missionaries to Brazil encountered Indians speaking tongues belonging to the *Tupí-Guaraní* language family, a form of this language was reduced to European script and used by them in their teaching. Indians whose native language was totally different were taught this *língua geral* (general language) and it soon became the language most commonly used by the newly-formed Brazilian peasant of the region. As late as the second half of the nineteenth century, it was spoken 'along the main Amazon for a distance of 2,500 miles' [2]. Near large towns and cities, it was used indiscriminately with Portuguese, but in the more

---

[1] The figures in brackets refer to the bibliography on page 141.

distant areas of the Valley *língua geral* was the only language known [3]. It was because of the widespread use of this language, and because of the physical appearance of the people, that most nineteenth-century foreign visitors spoke so often of 'Indian customs' and 'native life' when describing the small communities along the Amazon. What they describe, however, are old Iberian traditions, sometimes fused with aboriginal custom. They speak of the 'strange rite of crossing one self [4]'; of the celebrations and processions on Saints' days [5]; of the old Iberian Catholic custom of ritual godparenthood (*compadresco* system), and of granting children 'a blessing' in good Luso-Brazilian style.

These so-called 'Indians' lived mainly by Luso-Brazilian culture patterns and were already members of the regional society, serving as rubber collectors, canoemen, agricultural labourers, workers in domestic and public service, and members of the armed forces. Since the nineteenth century, these Amazon peasants, or *caboclos* as they are apt to be called, have been brought into increasingly closer touch with regional and national life. *Língua geral* has been replaced by Portuguese throughout the Valley, except in a very few isolated localities. Nowadays the rural *caboclos* discuss national and state politics, and if semi-literate they vote. They are Catholics, and the annual celebration of the patron saint of their community is a major event; September and other civic holidays of Brazil are celebrated by these rural Amazon people as they are elsewhere. They play *futebol*, or soccer, which is Brazil's national sport. The legal and political institutions, the educational system, and many other aspects of their social life are those of the nation. They are not 'Indians' but rural Brazilians, and much that may be said about rural life in the Amazon Valley might also be said about rural life in other parts of Brazil.

Yet the Indian has left an indelible mark upon Amazon rural life. Most of the methods used today in exploiting the environment are of Indian origin; the slash-and-burn farming methods, the techniques and lore used in hunting and fishing, and the knowledge of the products of the tropical forest which are collected for sale, are all derived from the Indian heritage. Innumerable Indian folk beliefs persist alongside those of Iberian origin; and in the rural neighbourhoods, even in the working-class districts of large cities, medicine men called by the *língua geral* term of *pagé* treat and perform cures by old Indian magical methods.

The Indian was the predominant element in the physical make-up of the Amazon population. In contrast with other regions of Brazil where the Indian was early eliminated as an active element, the American Indian has here continued to be an important element in society. While people of Amerind physical characteristics are not numerous in other regions of Brazil, the *caboclo* or *tapuia* (both terms

119

used for people of Indian racial type) are an important element to be considered in a study of race relations in the Amazon Valley.

II. Any one community in rural Amazon would serve our purpose for a 'case study' of the relations between racial groups. Any one community would give us a picture, however, of but a local manifestation of a set of patterns and institutions which are regional in scope, and no one community would provide us with the full range of inter-racial situations, and the institutions which determine such relations. But it is in the community that people make a living, that they educate their children, that they worship, and that face-to-face relations among people of different occupations, social classes and racial characteristics take place. It is in the local community that one may observe the way people of different racial characteristics live together and react to one another. This article will therefore focus upon community, while relating the observations on this one town to the wider regional situation.

This community, which is called by the fictitious name of Itá, is a small town situated on the southern banks of the Amazon mainstream, in the sub-region of the Valley (between Manaus and Belém) known generally as Lower Amazon. There are many others in the same sub-region which are more prosperous, larger in population, and more progressive. The way of life in Itá and in the surrounding countryside might seem old-fashioned to city people of the Amazon region, even to the people of larger towns such as Santarém. But the way of Itá is still that of the majority of the rural inhabitants of the Valley.

Itá has a long history. It was established in the early seventeenth century and has felt the influence of most of the trends of Amazon history. It is a poor community. There is no special industry based on natural gifts, and the economic life of the people is still based on slash-and-burn subsistence agriculture and on the collection of rubber and other forest products. It is a small town with less than 600 people, and the centre for a rural community of about 1,500 more. All three racial stocks which have formed the population of the Amazon, and all possible mixtures of the Causacoid, the Amerind and the Negro, are present in the population.

Race mixture in the population of the community of Itá has progressed to the point where any system of classification by racial groups is bound to be subjective or highly arbitrary. There are numerous individuals who list ancestors of all three racial stocks in their family tree, and there are others who combine physical traits generally thought of as Caucasoid, Negro and Amerind. Many people have the brown skin colouring, the narrow eyes and high cheek bones characteristic of the American Indian; but also the very

120

woolly hair of the Negro and the fine nose and lips which are considered to be Caucasoid traits. And there are individuals in Itá who are apparently pure Caucasoid, American Indian or Negro, at least from their physical appearance, though it would be impossible to affirm that even these extremes are genetically pure Caucasoid, Indian, or Negroid. Our general observations in Itá led us to believe that the American Indian physical type and genetic strain predominated over the other two stocks, but it also led us to beware of any attempt to classify accurately this highly mixed population in terms of racial groups.

Yet, perhaps because the physical types in the Itá population shade so imperceptibly into each other, forming a gradient rather than clear-cut groups based on physical traits, the people of Itá are unusually conscious of physical traits, and they themselves use a system of classifying people by physical types which is implicit in their everyday vocabulary and explicit in the minds of most of them.

In Itá, as elsewhere the term *branco* (white) is used for those of predominantly Caucasoid features; *moreno* (brunet) for those of mixed ancestry of almost any variety; *caboclo* or *tapuia* for those with the physical features of the American Indian; and *preto* (Negro) for those who are clearly Negroid. The term *mulato*, which is used in so widespread a fashion throughout Brazil, is only used in Itá in the feminine gender to refer to an attractive woman (e.g., *mulatinha bonita:* pretty girl; and *mulata boa:* literally a 'good mulatto', but implying sexual attractiveness as in 'attractive wench').

The term *negro* is seldom heard, and then only in anger; in a quarrel with anyone who has physical traits suggesting Negroid ancestry, the label '*negro ruim*' (bad Negro) is a powerful insult. The term *pardo*—which is so often used in Brazilian newspapers and in official census data to include people of various racial mixtures who are not clearly Negroid, Amerind, or Caucasoid—is not used in Itá except by a few government officials; the category of *moreno*, as used in Itá, is sufficiently broad and all-inclusive to cover all such types. In fact, people are classed as *moreno* whenever there is any doubt about their proper category. Sometimes a *preto* (Negro) or a *caboclo* (Indian) is called a *moreno* to his face or in speaking of him to his friends, to avoid any slight offence. Generally, however, such terms are used freely in describing one's friends and neighbours, much as one might speak of a blond or a brunet in European society; '*aquêle branco*' (that white) or '*aquêle preto* (that Negro) who lives near João Gomes', and so on, are typical ways in which people make use of these descriptive categories.

Skin colour is an important criterion in classifying people by 'racial' type in Itá, as it is in other parts of the world, but it is not the most decisive or the most frequent one. More important in Itá are the quality of the hair and the amount of body hair; and physiognomical characteristics such as the shape of the nose, fullness of the lips, and width of the face at the cheekbones are about equally noticed along with the colour of the skin.

The *branco* (white) for example, is thought as an individual with a heavy beard and fine straight hair. The *moreno* (brunet) has black straight or wavy hair, and less body hair than the *branco*. The *morena's* (i.e., the woman of mixed racial descent) long black tresses are considered specially attractive. The *caboclo* has thick coarse hair which (in men) 'stands on end despite all efforts to comb it'. But the black but coarse hair of the female *cabocla* is similar to that of the mixed *morena*, and is considered very attractive. Much fun is made of the *caboclo's* beard. 'He has three hairs on his chin', people say, and his attempts at a moustache generally result in but a few drooping strands. Similarly, the hair of the Negro is thought to be easily distinguished. The Negro has hair described as *pixaim* (kinky) or *pimenta do reino* (literally, black pepper)—terms used to indicate tightly-rolled kinky hair. People also laugh and say that 'the Negro has "break-a-comb" hair'. They tell the story of a well-known Negro musician whose presence at a rural dance might be known from his habit of stopping along the river to bathe before arriving; as he combed his hair after his bath, the ring of the teeth of his aluminium comb might be heard at a distance by the waiting dancers at the festival.

Other features such as thick lips which are the sign of Negroid ancestry, high cheekbones and slant eyes which are characteristics pointing to Indian ancestry, and even skin colour, are often mentioned as characteristics of the various 'racial' categories; but people explain that skin colour and other physical traits are not trustworthy criteria. 'They fool one', explained several people in Itá, who give more credence to hair as a deciding trait.

The distribution of the population in the Itá community according to race can only be estimated in general terms. Classifications of people in terms of their physical characteristics tend, as will be shown later, to be confused with their social position. But 202 adults in the community, who were included in a detailed house-to-house survey, were classified with the help of our local assistants by their physical characteristics, according to the fourfold classification used in Itá. Of these 102, or slightly over 50 per cent, were classed as *moreno;* 34, or slightly less than 17 per cent, as *branco;* 47, or slightly over 23 per cent, as *caboclo;* and only 19, or slightly less than 10 per cent, as *preto.* This estimate of the distribution of the population by racial groups substantially agrees with a census, made independently by the Public Health authorities, of 305 people of Itá, which classed 218, or 71 per cent, as *pardo* (seemingly including those who might also be classed as *caboclo*); 57, or 19 per cent, as *branco*; and 30, or 10 per cent, as *preto.* Neither of these estimates can be considered

122

scientifically objective, since they reflect the particular bias of the classifiers (i.e., of the anthropologists[1] and their local assistants in the former, and of the Public Health officer in the latter) and their awareness of certain phenotypical physical characteristics. But the two estimates do give a general idea of the appearance of the Itá population.

III. Certain stereotyped concepts regarding the behaviour of people in accordance with their physical type have persisted in Itá from the colonial period, and reflect the different social position of the three racial stocks in colonial society. As indicated above, values of physical attractiveness are implicit in the very categories used. As in other parts of Brazil, people speak of 'good hair' (straight and fine) or 'bad hair' (curly to kinky). The light complexion and the fine features of the Caucasoid (*branco*) are considered the most attractive. Mothers sometimes boast of the thin nose, the light skin, and the fine hair of their children. But people actually lean toward the *moreno* and the *morena* in their ideals of beauty and physical attractiveness. Men find the *morena*, which they identify as a dark brunette or even a very brown mulatto, to be the most attractive feminine type. They like the long straight hair of the *tapuia* woman, the regular and fine features of the *branca*, and the large brown eyes, the dark complexion, and the black hair of the woman of mixed ancestry. These features are often combined in the *morena*, whose ancestry is apt to be a combination of three racial stocks.

On the other hand, women prefer lighter men with 'good' (straight) hair and Caucasoid features. In Colonial times, it was to the advantage of the Indian or Negro woman to marry, or to become the concubine of, a European, and even today most of the men holding bureaucratic positions and owning property are *brancos*, so that the woman's preferences are closely tied to economic and social factors. Emilia, a young girl of Luso-Indian descent, was quite blunt about her preference and even about the reasons for it: 'I would not marry a *preto*', she said, 'even if he were perfumed.' She would have liked to marry a 'light *moreno*', but she found a very dark mulatto, who was a successful business man, 'very attractive'. She said that 'although he is too dark, he has money'. Many women mentioned Marcos Dias, the dark *moreno* son of the *preto* Alfredo Dias, as a

[1] The group which carried out the field study in Itá was composed of three Brazilians from Rio de Janeiro and one North American. The classification by racial type was first made by a local assistant, who was himself classed as a *moreno*, and then checked by a member of our field party, keeping in mind as far as possible the local criteria for racial types. In many cases, our own classification would have tended to increase the number of Negroes and American Indians, since all of us seemed to emphasize skin colour. The Public Health physician responsible for the second estimate was a Brazilian from the south, but this survey was actually performed by a field inspector who was born and educated in the Amazon Valley.

very handsome man, despite 'his (dark) colour and his bad (kinky) hair'. These ideals of physical attractiveness which persist in Itá were conditioned by the social system of the Colonial period; the physical features of the dominant Europeans are those which are, in general, most higly valued, and those of the Indian and the Negro are less desirable. But just as the Portuguese colonist found the dark woman (the Indian and the mulatto) beautiful, these dark beauties also found it to their advantage to be sought by the lighter male.

The fixed ideas which the people of Itá maintain regarding the innate abilities of people of each 'racial' category also reflect the position of each of these groups in Colonial society. In Itá, people say that the *branco* is always 'good at business', and a man who is physically a *branco* arriving in the community would be considered *per se* 'intelligent and well educated'—obviously a persistence from the time when most Europeans were landed aristocrats, owners of great rubber-producing forests, or important officials from the capital. Our informants in Itá told us with some amusement of strangers who were *brancos* but who came dressed in poor clothes and who were found to be illiterate. In asking for a favour, people in Itá are apt to address others as '*Meu branco*'! (My white!), a term indicating high respect.

As in other parts of Brazil—and, for that matter, other parts of the New World—people of mixed Negro and Caucasoid parentage (the *moreno* of Itá and the mulatto of other regions) are considered treacherous, irascible, and difficult to deal with. Especially those with light skin, 'who seem almost *branco*', are thought to have *mau gênio* (literally, bad character)—a term used to indicate an irritable person whose mood shifts easily to anger, and not to describe a person's moral character. No one in Itá liked one of the Public Health physicians, a dark mulatto who spent some time there waiting for a boat to take him to his post. At first, several families invited him to visit them and men sought him out for conversation, since being a doctor he was a visitor of considerable prestige. But people soon found him to be abrupt and aggressive. He was critical of Itá, complaining that it was a dull town. The attitude of the townspeople soon changed. 'When a dark *moreno* becomes a doctor,' one man said, 'he is proud and he tries to act like a white.' People will overlook their fixed concepts of the different physical types, but when there is any reason to criticize a person they soon fall back upon these concepts to justify their feelings.

The number and variety of the stereotypes held in Itá in regard to the *preto* seem strangely out of keeping with the small number of Negroes in the present population and with the relatively small contribution of the African to the present way of life. There is a veritable aura of prestige tied to the 'old Negroes' (*os velhos pretos*, as they are called). It was a group of 'old Negroes', people say, who

124

were the leaders in the famous brotherhood devoted to Saint Benedict, the most famous and most miraculous saint of the whole Lower Amazon area. This brotherhood was able to raise large sums of money and the devotion to their saint drew, as it does today, thousands of people for the saint's annual festival. It was the great devotion and the ability of these 'old Negroes' which made the brotherhood of Saint Benedict in Itá such a strong one; 'the old Negroes began to die and the "whites" began to take part in the devotion to Saint Benedict' is the way in which people of all racial groups explain the relative decadence and disorganization of Saint Benedict's brotherhood today. Furthermore, the small village of Jocojó, which is a part of the Itá community, is said to have been inhabited almost entirely by 'old Negroes', although the people living there today have about the same appearance as the rest of the people of the area. This, explains people in Itá, is why the annual festival of São Pedro is always so well celebrated in Jocojó, and why the brotherhood devoted to this local saint is still so strong. 'It is due to the knowledge and the devotion of the "old Negroes of Jocojó",' people say.

The *preto* is also known as a fluent conversationalist and a good story-teller. People say that the 'old Negroes' who lived in Itá over a generation ago knew more stories than anyone else and told them better, and a local saying has it that 'whoever talks a lot is a Negro'. Maria, the light *morena* who is the wife of Juca, is an excellent story-teller, and people directed us to her at once when they heard that we were interested in hearing traditional legends and myths of the Amazon. 'She (Maria) tells so many stories that she is almost a *preta*', we were told. Others who told us stories would often say that they had heard them from an 'old Negro' who was long since dead. And they pointed to Roque, a very black *preto* who was very articulate about his experiences as a rubber gatherer in the upper reaches of the Amazon tributaries, and who indeed told stories very well, as an example of the Negro story-teller. People excused Roque's somewhat doubtful veracity by saying that he was a '*preto* who liked to talk'.

In Itá the Negro is known, in addition, as witty and crafty; and the Negro male is thought of as especially potent sexually. He has large genitalia and is therefore thought to be much appreciated by women of all racial groups. A series of pornographic stories told in Itá among men illustrate all these qualities of the Negro. In several of these stories, he is having a sexual affair with a white woman, the wife of his master—or of his *patrão* (boss) if the story is placed in modern times. The stories revolve around the skill of the Negro in tricking his master or *patrão*, who suspects the affair but is unable to discover the pair together. Men tell of the sexual exploits of *pretos* of their acquaintance and of their greater sexual abilities. The Negro woman

125

and the dark *morena* are also considered to have greater sexual appetites than the *cabocla* or the white woman. But the craftiness of the Negro is not limited to situations involving his sexual exploits. There are stories of how the *preto* outsmarted his master who would punish him for not working, and how the Negro equalized matters with a trader *patrão* who overcharged him for the goods he purchased.

The stereotypes of the Negro as a good story-teller, and especially as potent sexually, are similar to stereotypes regarding the Negro encountered in North America. The same sort of joke, many of which are pornographic, are told in the North American South about the Negro [6]. Undoubtedly, these similar stereotypes result from the background of Negro slavery which is common both to southern North America and to northern Brazil. But here the similarity ends. The picture of the 'old Negro' as a good story-teller in Itá is not that of Uncle Remus who mildly recounts folk-tales to a younger audience. In Itá, the picture evoked is that of the colourful raconteur of stories of all kinds, both 'for the family' and for the ears of men in the bar.

The stereotype of the sexual ability of the Negro male may well arise from sexual envy on the part of non-Negro males in Itá, as it seems to in the south of the United States. But it does not serve, as Gunnar Myrdal indicates for the North American south, 'as part of the social control devices to aid in preventing intercourse between Negro males and white females' [7]. This very situation is part of the plot of many pornographic stories, and both legal marriages and extra-marital sexual affairs between Negro males and lighter females are commonplace occurences in Itá. Nor do the stories told about the Negro serve the function of 'proving (his) inferiority' [8], but on the contrary they tend to illustrate a superior quality, namely his craftiness. In Itá these stories are not told by a white caste about an inferior caste—they are stories told by people of various racial hues about their fellow-citizens. In Itá, the stereotypes held in regard to the Negro show him on the whole in a favourable light. To be sure, *they show the Negro as inferior to the white*, but he has many attributes which are highly valued in Itá society.

Yet, at the same time, people in Itá, disparage the Negro, if in a rather warm and humorous manner. They know and make use of widespread Brazilianisms which disparage and belittle him, such as 'if the Negro does not soil when he enters, he does when he leaves', and many others which are reported by Donald Pierson in his excellent study of race relations in urban Bahia, and by the authors of accompanying papers in this volume. But these sayings are apt to be used by *pretos* about themselves, and by people in a light joking manner to chide their intimate friends of obvious Negro ancestry. Juca, for example, whose mother was a well-known 'old Negro', often blamed his own bad habits on his Negro ancestry. 'I talk too much because I am a *preto*', he said to the amusement of his visitors. 'I would put an end to that race of people (the Negro)' he 'ad-libbed' into the lines of a folk play in which he had an important part, 'but the devil of it, I also come from the same quality.' Juca's complaints about his Negro ancestry always brought laughter, for people knew that he was proud of his mother. No one in Itá, to our knowledge, is ashamed of Negroid ancestry, and the prestige of the 'old Negroes' is high in Itá tradition.

The stereotypes which the people of Itá hold regarding the *tapuia* or the *caboclo* (American Indian physical types), on the other hand, are not as favourable as for the Negro. The *caboclo* appears as a good hunter and fisherman. He has a special sensitivity for the habits of animals and he knows almost instinctively where and how to hunt or fish. No one can remember a famous hunter who was not a '*caboclo* with but three hairs on his chin'. Elias Veiga, a man of 65 years of age, was known in his earlier years as an excellent hunter. He was born and raised in the rural district near Itá where he learned very early to hunt, but people attribute his skill to the fact that 'he is a *tapuia*' (i.e., of American Indian physical type). These concepts are harmless enough, for skill at hunting is something useful and admired.

Still, *caboclo* and *tapuia* are in a sense terms of disparagement; people do not use them when speaking directly to people of Indian physical characteristics. 'It is not a hard word,' said Elias Veiga who was pointed out as a typical representative of this physical type, 'but it makes a person sad.'

In Itá, as throughout the Amazon Valley, the term has a double meaning—one indicating low social status, and another indicating Indian physical characteristics. People in Amazon cities often use the term *caboclo* when referring to the rural peasant of the interior; upper-class people in Itá dismiss all people below them as *caboclos;* while the people of low social status and people like Elias Veiga use the term for the savage tribal Indians who live in the headwaters of the Amazon tributaries. Furthermore, most of the stereotypes associated with the *caboclo* or the *tapuia* are derogatory. The *caboclo* is considered lazy—'they do not plant gardens but live on the sale of a little rubber and by fishing for their meals'. The *caboclo* is thought to be timid because he lives isolated in the forest; people say he prefers to live 'like an animal' (*como um bicho*) away from others, deep in the forest. He is thus unused to the social life of a town; humorous stories are told picturing him in the role of a ridiculous hick whose feet are swollen by the hard ground of the town ('he is accustomed to the soft mud of the swamps') and by the unaccustomed shoes which he wears in town. People told us how the *caboclo* who comes to town to attend a festival finally takes off his shoes to carry them

127

over his shoulder, and how he retires to a hammock to rest his swollen feet. At festivals no one wants to dance with him, as he treads on his partner's feet. People also point out the numerous marriages ordered by the police among *caboclos* who live in the rural areas—where the groom has to be threatened by the girl's father or by the police to go through with the ceremony—as evidence of their lower moral standards.

The *caboclo*, is thought to be tricky and exceedingly suspicious. A popular local saying has it that 'the suspicious *caboclo* hangs up his hammock and then sleeps under it' (i.e., he suspects that even the hammock he has hung for himself will fall). Commercial men say that the *caboclo* must be watched in any business deal; he will insert a rock in the core of a large ball of crude rubber to increase its weight when he sells it to the trader. He will sell to the unsuspecting trader *timborana*, a vine which resembles the true *timbó* from which insecticides are produced, but which has no value. Such stereotypes regarding the *caboclo* are not limited to people of that physical type (American Indian) but are often aimed at all rural rubber collectors. As most people point out, these collectors are in their great majority *tapuias* or *caboclos* in a physical sense, but even town dwellers of this physical type are thought to share their timidity, laziness, ability at hunting and fishing, and trickiness.

People of Indian descent, unlike those of Negroid descent, do not like to be reminded of their Indian ancestry. The children playing in front of an Itá home were heard many times teasing the housewife, of *caboclo* physical type. They called her *tapuia* and *índia*, and she would reply in anger: 'Go away, your parents are Indians themselves.' In the Amazon, the Indian, even more often than the Negro, was the slave in colonial times. The few Negroes who arrived in Itá and other communities up-river from the delta region must have already been freemen, or the exceedingly valuable property of wealthy landowners who treated them with more care than their Indian slaves and peons. In the opinion of the European, the Indian was a nude barbarian of less prestige than the more expensive African. Today, Indian physical characteristics are therefore not only a symbol of slave ancestry, but of a social origin in colonial times lower than the Negro's.

IV. These fixed ideas and concepts which the people of Itá hold regarding people of different physical characteristics obviously reflect a system of social ranking. The *branco* and the *moreno* are the preferred physical types. The *preto* is highly respected, although not considered physically attractive. The *caboclo*, although not considered unattractive physically, has characteristics which place him low in the social scale. It is therefore obvious that physical race is related to social rank. The way in which the people of Itá conceive the relations between racial groups, however, must be understood in terms of the entire system of social ranking, which involves other factors in addition to physical appearance. In fact, the people of Itá, when asked to classify their fellow townspeople in accordance with their physical characteristics into one of the four categories (*branco*, *moreno*, *preto* and *caboclo*), were apt to fuse the social position of the individual with his or her physical traits.

Eleven informants were asked to classify 20 well-known individuals according to physical type. The town drunk, the leader of the annual *Boi Bumbá* folk drama, the schoolteacher, a well-known employee at the town hall, the rich widow who was the owner of the largest commercial house, and others equally well known to everyone were included in the list. There was general agreement among our informants as to the physical classification of those people on the list whose physical characteristics were clearly Negroid or Caucasoid. For example Alfredo Dias, the pilot of a motor launch stationed at Itá, whose hair, facial features and black skin clearly placed him as a Negro, was classified at once as a *preto* by nine people, although two people thought that he should be called a *moreno* despite his marked physical traits. Agreement was also fairly general when the physical appearance of an individual coincided with his social position. The adopted son of a wealthy widow was classified by 10 people as *branco* and by only one as *moreno*. He has a light complexion, fine features, and a heavy beard, and is known in town as an astute businessman.

On the other hand, people did not agree on the racial classification of those on the list whose physical traits were not so clear-cut, who were obviously of mixed racial descent, or whose physical appearance conflicted with their expected social position. Thus, in classifying the schoolteacher, five people classed her as a *branca*, probably somewhat influenced by her social position, and six found her to be a *morena*, probably because of her rather brunette complexion and her hair texture. The vice-mayor of Itá, who was also an important commercial man, was classified by three people as *branco*, by three as *caboclo*, and by five as *moreno*. He is a rather portly man whose mixed ancestry is clearly of all three racial stocks, but his appearance is more that of an Indian-Caucasoid *mestiço*.

The town drunk was called a *caboclo* by five people despite his obvious Caucasoid features, which the other six took into consideration in calling him a *branco*. 'How can Oswaldo be a *branco*?' one informant exclaimed, referring to his low social position. Conversely, Dona Dora Cesar Andrade, the widow mentioned above, the owner of the largest commercial house in Itá and the person who might perhaps be said to have the highest prestige in town, was classed as a *morena* by nine people and as a *branca* by two. Dona Dora is a dark mula'to with fine facial features and relatively long, but wavy, hair. One of our Itá informants explained that Dona Dora had a white father and a Negro mother, 'but her money whitens her skin'. He implied that if Dona Dora were lower in social rank she might even be classed as a *preta*. This conflict between racial characteristics and the expected social position reminds one of the Brazilian expression, 'a rich Negro is a white man and a poor white is a Negro', as well as the much-cited story related by the nineteenth century English traveller, Henry Koster. During his travels, Koster inquired of a man of colour who was in his service whether a certain high official was not a 'mulatto'. He received the following reply: 'He was, but he is not now.' Koster asked for further explanation and his servant added: 'Can a *Capitam-mór* be a mulatto?' [9].

In Itá, as in all human societies, the system of ranking individuals in a prestige series depends upon a combination of factors. Physical appearance is but one of several which determine one's social position. Because Itá is a small and isolated community, the distance between the lowest and the highest individuals in the social scale is not so great as in large cities and in communities with more complex social structures. In fact, from the point of view of the outsider, Itá might seem to be a community of homogeneous rural peasants with a few government officials and commercial people of slightly higher social rank. People from the city of Belém pay visits to the Public Health doctor, the only person in the community with a secondary or professional, education; to Dona Dora; to the Mayor, who in 1948 was a young man who had once been a sailor in the Brazilian navy; or to the state and federal tax collectors who are city people from Belém temporarily stationed in Itá. Such people might be roughly classed with the 'middle class' of the city. At the same time, visitors have been heard to marvel at the high social and economic position of Dona Dora, 'who is only a dark *mulata*', and to say that the Mayor 'is nothing but a *caboclo*'. Outsiders recognize that the Itá community does not include any members of the regional aristocracy (the aristocratic landholding families, the professional class, the commercial and industrial group, and the political leaders who form the current upper class of the Amazon region).

There was a time, however, when the range of social ranking was greater in the Itá community. In the first centuries of the town's history, those who were born of Indian or mixed Indian-European parents lived in general in the *aldeia* (village) district of the town, while the Europeans and the more Europeanized *mestiços* lived in the *cidade* (city), as the European districts of Amazon towns were called [10].

In the early colonial society there were two castes: those who were either slave- or peon-born (usually of Indian physical type) and

130

those who were born as freemen of the governing caste, usually of European physical characteristics. As slavery disappeared, as the process of incorporation of the Indian into regional life continued in the Amazon and as miscegenation increased, people of Indian-Caucasoid parentage took their place on the lower rungs of the European caste. As these processes have continued, physical appearance counts less and less in distinguishing the two groups.

In Itá, as in most of northern Brazil, the social distinctions originally based on the difference between slaves and landowning slave-owners, between Negroes or Indians and Europeans, continued into the twentieth century in the form of rigidly divided social classes. During the rubber boom, in the first decade of this century, the wealth derived from native rubber increased the social distance between the rich rubber merchants and the miserably poor rubber collectors—although, as in most booms, individuals from the lower class sometimes 'struck it rich' and moved into the upper stratum. In these prosperous times, there was an 'aristocracy' in Itá. Families, such as that of the Baron of Itá (a member of the 'nobility of the Empire' created by Pedro II of Brazil) actually resided there. Such families were proud of their Portuguese ancestry, educated their children in the large cities of Brazil and even of Europe, were wealthy in land, and participated actively in the political and social life of the region. A member of the lower classes in Itá in those days would not have dared sit down in the presence of one of these 'aristocrats'; whenever there was a festival there would be two rooms for dancers—one for the 'families' or upper class, and another for the 'people' or lower class.

After the rubber crash and during the period of general decadence throughout the Amazon, which followed, the town of Itá declined in population. Many of the commercial houses in the town and in the surrounding area went bankrupt. Most of the 'aristocracy' moved away. Nowadays, only a few descendants of this upper class remain in Itá, and these few are impoverished and without the educational and economic advantages of their ancestors. Social differences between the 'aristocracy' and the 'people' are no longer as rigidly delineated as they were in the past; and with the continued miscegenation among racial groups, racial type is no longer, as we shall see, as closely correlated with social position in Itá as it was in the past. Yet the people of Itá are still sensitive to differences in social rank. They are quite explicit about the fact that theirs is a society of several social strata, and not a homogeneous group of rural peasants.

The social strata in Itá society still reflect the rigid class lines of feudal Amazon society in the colonial period, and the former condition of servitude of the imported African slave and the native Indian. In their simplest form the social strata, as described by the people of Itá themselves, are, in order of their rank in the community: (a) the 'first class' (*gente de primeira*) or, as they also say in, Itá, 'the whites' (*os brancos*); (b) the 'second class' (*gente de segunda*) the lower-class townspeople; (c) the 'farmers' (*gente de sítio*), who are the subsistence agriculturalists inhabiting the highlands in the vicinity of Itá, and (d) the island collectors (*seringueiros*) or the *caboclos de beira* (*caboclos* of the river banks), who live in houses built on stilts in the low-lying islands and in the swamp land near Itá. Not everyone in Itá is aware of all four of these social strata. The people belonging to the highest in rank—the 'first class'— sometimes classify all others lower than their restricted group simply as *caboclos*. But the lower-class people of the town (the 'second class') feel superior to the 'farmers', and the latter declare their superiority to the collectors.

The lines of social cleavage, however, are most carefully drawn between the 'first class' and the three lower strata. It is perhaps proper, then, to speak of Itá as a society with but two social classes— an upper class composed of the 'first class', and a lower class consisting of the 'second class', the 'farmer' and the collector. In our studies of standards of living, of education, and of other socio-economic factors, it was between these two classes that the most marked differences were noted. Between the three lower strata of the lower class, differences in income, expenditure, educational level and housing facilities were not great. Furthermore, it is relatively easy for a collector to move into the agricultural zone of the Itá community and thus in time to be accepted as a 'farmer'; and the farmer or the collector may move to town and soon be accepted by the people as a lower-class townsdweller, a member of the 'second class'. To move from any of these lower strata into the 'first class', however, is almost impossible In all of the personal histories which were recorded in Itá, only one case is known of an individual who raised his social status from one of the lower strata to the upper class. This was the case of a man who had been adopted by a wealthy commercial man and who had then married his foster father's daughter to take over the business. The other successful men of whom we were told had all climbed in the social hierarchy by moving to other communities where they were not known.

On the basis of our census in Itá, we are able to estimate that approximately 10 per cent of the people of the community (almost one-third of the townspeople) are classified as 'first class'; about 20 per cent (two-thirds of the population of the town) as 'second class'; about 60 per cent as 'farmers'; and only 10 per cent as 'collectors', since the bulk of these people live outside the community zone of which Itá is the centre. In other words, 10 per cent of the people of Itá are 'upper class' and 90 per cent belong to one of the three strata of the lower class. The criteria used by our local informants in helping us place people in their proper social strata were multiple;

some of them were explicit and others implicit, only to be derived from further study of the families after they had been classified for us.

An explicit criterion was occupation. Physical labour, in the nineteenth century and before, was limited to the slave-peon caste and to those recently freed. With the end of slavery, manual labour has continued as a symbol of low social status. Of the 17 men who were classed as 'first class' in our household survey, none worked with their hands; of 96 men classified in one of the three lower strata, all but two (clerks in the town hall) earned their living from some form of manual labour. The very few artisans, such as the shoemaker and the carpenters, were classed as 'second class town dwellers'.

Standard-of-living also was an explicit criterion. The average cash income of upper-class families was approximately $75.00 (Cr.$1,597.10) per month, as against an average of $21.25 (Cr.$425.00) for the three lower strata taken as a group. Expenditures for food and household necessities also differ strikingly between the two classes. 'First class' families in our survey spent approximately $48.00 (Cr.$962.20) per month for food and household necessities, while the average for the lower groups was but $14.30 (Cr.$286.40) per month.[1] Furthermore, the differences in standard of living between the two classes was indicated by the kind of food they ate, the clothes they wore, and the houses in which they lived. All the rural lower class, and three-fourths of the town's lower strata lived in 'huts' (*barracas*) made of clay or palm-thatched walls and thatched roofs. All 'first class' families lived in structures classed as 'houses' (*casas*), which are more permanent structures with thick adobe walls, floors, and a ceramic roof. Within the town, the 'second class' huts are situated on 'Third Street' back from the river front, while the upper-class houses are on 'First Street' facing the river, or on 'Second Street' near the public *praça* (plaza or square).

In addition to these material criteria, education is an important factor in class position. While no one in the upper class has more than a few years of primary school, all of them are literate, but more than 80 per cent of the people in the entire municipality of Itá are illiterate.[2] Another non-material factor which tends to classify one as upper-class is 'family'. Not all the 'first class' people of Itá come from traditional families who have held wealth and position in the past, but the descendants of such families are all considered upper-

---

[1] These contrasts in cash income and expenditure are, of course, offset somewhat by the fact that lower-class families have gardens (22 out of the 52 men of the 'second class' and of the 'farmers' had them) and by the fact that most of them fish during the dry season for food. Upper-class people have no gardens and seldom fish.

[2] Data furnished for the year 1945 by the Instituto Brasileiro de Geografia e Estatística and based on the number of inhabitants above five years of age.

class in the community, despite the fact that some of them are nowadays quite poor. One's personal behaviour is also taken into consideration; a lower-class man removes his hat when talking to an upper-class man or woman; a person of the lower class hesitates to sit down in an upper-class home; and lower-class women are 'embarrassed' in front of 'upper-class people. These and other minutiae of behaviour denote lower-class status, and are noticed by people in Itá. Raimundo Gonçalves, for example, moved to Itá about five years ago. He came as a federal employee to supervise the work on an airport at Itá. His position gave him great prestige and he began to augment his salary by paying day labourers to plant large manioc gardens to produce manioc flour for sale. He is for Itá relatively high on the economic scale, and he and his family are Caucasoid in appearance. But Raimundo is considered lower-class. He is not illiterate, but his handwriting, his spelling, and his vocabulary mark him as a man with little schooling. Furthermore, he does manual work, working alongside the labourers on the airport and in his own garden. And, above all, both he and his wife are humble; they are shy in front of such people as Dona Dora or the federal tax collector. The people of Itá did not need a family genealogy to know that Raimundo and his wife are 'of the people'.

Physical appearance—racial type—is one, but only one, of these various criteria which, taken together, determine one's social status in Itá. As indicated above, there are people of all racial types in each of the various social strata. Social class is far from being closely correlated with racial type, as it must have been in early colonial times, but the old rule of the thumb which has been used for Brazil as a whole, 'the darker the skin, the lower the class', may be said to apply to Itá [11]. The majority of the Itá 'upper class' are of European racial type, or in local terms *brancos*. The term *branco* is used for both a racial type and for the upper class. The majority of the lower class are *mestiços* (mixtures of Caucasoid with Indian and/or Negro), Negroes or Amerindians in physical appearance. Table I gives the 'racial' classification of 202 Itá adults (the fathers and mothers of the families included in our detailed household survey) and their classification by social class. Of the 30 people who were classed as 'first class' (upper class) by our Itá informants, 53 per cent (or 16 individuals) were Caucasoid, at least in their general appearance; 44 per cent (or 13 individuals) were of mixed racial type, and were classed as *morenos* in the local system of racial classification; only 3 per cent (or one individual) had American Indian physical features and was classed physically as *caboclo*; and it is noteworthy that none were *pretos*. Of the 172 people placed in the three lower strata, only about 10 per cent (or 18 individuals) were of Caucasoid racial type; 51 per cent (or 89 individuals) were placed in the *moreno* category; 27 per cent (or 46 individuals) showed notable Indian physical charac-

134

TABLE I. Classification of 202 adults by race and by social class

Social strata	Branco No.	Branco %	Moreno No.	Moreno %	Caboclo No.	Caboclo %	Preto No.	Preto %	Total
MASCULINE									
Upper Class *Brancos* or 'First class'	7	50	6	42.9	1	7.1	—	—	14
Lower class Second class	4	8.7	25	54.4	10	21.7	7	15.2	46
Farmers	2	6.9	14	48.3	9	31	4	13.8	29
Collectors	2	22.2	4	44.5	2	22.2	1	11.1	9
TOTAL	15	15.3	49	50	22	22.5	12	12.2	98
FEMININE									
Upper Class *Brancos* or 'First class'	9	56.2	7	43.8	—	—	—	—	16
Lower Class Second class	5	9.6	27	52	14	26.9	6	11.5	52
Farmers	1	3.8	16	61.6	8	30.8	1	3.8	26
Collectors	4	40	3	30	3	30	—	—	10
TOTAL	19	183	53	51	25	24	7	6.7	104

teristics and were called *caboclos*; and 12 per cent (or 19 individuals) seemed to be *pretos*.[1]

These figures make it obvious, despite the numerous subjective judgments which must have figured in the classification of individuals, that the descendants of the Negro and the Indian continue

[1] See Table I for a breakdown of these figures according to the three social strata which make up the Itá lower class.

to occupy, as a whole, a low position in the Itá social hierarchy. These descendants of slaves have not been able to rise during the past century from the low social position at the bottom of the social ladder where they entered regional society. In Itá, the effects of mass education and other influences which would open up the possibility for social ascension to such people, have not been felt to any important degree. *Indian and Negro physical characteristics are a symbol of low social status and of slave ancestry.*

Yet it is also obvious from the figures cited above that there are no immutable barriers because of racial characteristics to prevent an individual from moving upward in the social hierarchy. A large percentage of those classified as 'first class' are of mixed racial descent and many of them are *mestiços* with marked Indian or Negroid features. As mentioned above, the wealthy widow, Dona Dora— the individual of perhaps highest prestige in town—is a dark *morena*, and her late husband, who was the town's most important commercial man and a recognized leader throughout the community, was a Negro. The Mayor of Itá in 1948, who was of course placed at once as a 'first class' member, had the copper skin colour, the straight black hair and the high cheekbones of the American Indian. Furthermore, 10 per cent of those classed as 'lower class' had Caucasoid physical features; the town drunk, who served as a porter carrying trunks from the boats that stopped at Itá, was always placed in the 'lower class', although he had a heavy red-blond beard and his skin colour was very light. In fact, a few people remember that his father came from Portugal.

There are numerous other cases of dark *mestiços* with high social rank, and people of Caucasoid appearance with low-class position. Social position is based upon economics, upon education, upon the family to which one belongs, as well as upon physical traits. *Physical race is but an uncertain symbol of one's social position and not an absolute determinant.* When physical appearance clashes with the social position of an individual, as in the cases mentioned above, social position tends to override observable physical traits. People find it difficult—as shown in our interviews mentioned above, during which they were asked to classify others by physical type—to call a high-placed person a *caboclo* or a *preto*, or to call an individual of low status a *branco*. In such cases, they tend to remember, even to see, physical traits which would place the individual as a racial type more in accord with their social rank. In extreme cases, such as that of the outstanding commercial man who was a Negro, where there is no doubt as to the individual's physical type, people are careful to explain: 'He is First Class although he is a Negro.' Social rank is beyond any doubt more important to the people of Itá than physical race.

V. Physical race, in fact, does not loom large in the daily lives of the people of Itá. There is no segragation of any kind in terms of physical characteristics. Children of all physical types attend both the town school and the few schools in the rural areas; children of all racial types and mixtures play freely together. The religious brotherhoods devoted to Saints, which are the principal formal associations in the community, include all physical types. Segregation by race is almost incomprehensible to people in Itá. One or two literate members of the community had heard stories of racial segregation in North America, but they found it difficult to believe, even when assured that it did in fact exist.[1]

People do not seem, furthermore, to select their friends on the basis of racial type. The stereotypes and the attitudes regarding the behaviour of people of different racial types, and the fact that people of various racial groups are roughly divided by class lines, does not seem to influence day-to-day social relations.

And yet, the emphasis upon social rank in Itá and the fact that people of Indian and Negro ancestry are still generally of low social rank, produces an effect which in a measure resembles 'race segregation'. Since the lower-class townspeople live mainly on 'Third Street' back from the river, people of Negro and Indian physical type live mainly together there. The government officials who are 'first class' and who are, most of them, of apparent Caucasoid physical type, live on the other hand on 'First Street' (facing the river) or near the main public square, which are the two most desirable residential districts.

At any party or dance offered by the Mayor, or at a luncheon or reception for a visiting notable, the outside visitor might have the impression that racial segregation was at work in determining the list of people invited. True, Dona Dora, the wealthy widow, and perhaps the river pilot, who is a Negro, as well as the Mayor, Vice-Mayor, and others of mixed racial descent, would certainly be present, but the group attending such a party would, on the whole, be lighter in pigmentation and more Caucasoid in appearance than the general population. Again, people in Itá seek mates of approximately the same physical type. Of 82 married couples known to us, 56 couples were of the same physical type—that is, both *brancos*, or both *pretos*, and so forth. The other 26 couples in which man and wife were classified in different physical categories were marriages between people of those categories which were nearest in pigmentation. They were all marriages of a *branco* with a *moreno*, a dark

---

[1] One man, a judge from a neighbouring town, had heard that there was a district of New York surrounded by barbed wire in which the Negroes lived. He had been convinced that this was true but was unable to convince others, who would not believe that such a district as Harlem existed even without the 'barbed wire'.

moreno with a *preto*, or a *preto* with a *caboclo*. There were no marriages, in our sample, between a *preto* and a *branco*.

These marriages between people of the same physical type or of approximately the same colour are not determined by any restrictions against inter-racial marriages. They result from the fact that people tend to marry roughly within the same social stratum. Since people of one stratum tend to be of similar physical type, marriage in one's own stratum means marriage between people roughly similar in physical type. That marriages between people of different physical type are not prohibited, not even discouraged, was attested by our Itá informants, who remembered numerous cases of *branco* men marrying women of Indian or Negro physical type and of *pretos* and *caboclos* marrying *branco* wives. Whatever segregation exists is based on class rather than race.

It cannot however be said that racial or colour prejudice is totally absent. The numerous unfavourable stereotypes regarding the *caboclo* and the *preto* certainly indicate a form, no matter how mild, of prejudice. Yet, as also mentioned above, people are overt and rather humorous about their having such invidious attitudes. They will speak of their parents, with great affection, as 'a *caboclo* who would trust no one', or as 'an old Negro who was devoted to Saint Benedict'. Others call themselves a *tapuia* or 'nothing but a *preto*', although they might not like it if others did. Never have we heard of any overt tensions arising in Itá between people on the basis of racial differences. There was occasional persecution of the Moroccan Jewish merchants who established themselves there during the rubber boom, but this seems to have been due to differences in custom and religion, or to political reasons. Several men told us that it was a sport of youthful drinking companions to 'give the *hebraicos* a beating' and one man recounted with some gaiety the story of the sacking of a Jewish-owned store around 1908. They were not Catholics; they spoke Portuguese with an accent; they closed their stores on Saturday; they had their own cemetery; they would not marry Brazilians—these were the reasons advanced for such antagonism.

Yet these Jews were considered as upper-class, and as *branco* in physical type. Two of them became Mayors of Itá, and everyone in town is proud of the famous physician in Belém who was born in Itá of Jewish parents. The attacks on the Jews were part of the frequent violence connected with the intense political feelings of the times—the sacking of the Jewish store was, according to several informants, instigated by a politician whom the store-owner was opposing in the elections. Today, the one remaining family of Jewish merchants live as an integrated part of the community. Dona Deborah, a widow who was born abroad and brought up and married as an orthodox Jew, feels a nostalgia for people who understand her

138

beliefs and way of life. Her sons have all married Brazilians of Catholic faith, and her daughter, who married the son of a Jewish immigrant to Brazil, had left her husband and was living at home. Within a little more than one generation, the few Jewish newcomers are about to be absorbed into Itá society.[1]

While physical characteristics do not provide any serious barrier to social mobility, they make it more difficult. The fixed concepts of expected behaviour according to physical type tend to limit the possibilities of people with regard to occupation—an individual of Indian-physical type would be accepted sooner than others as a river boatman, 'because the *caboclo* knows the channels in the river', and a Negro would be hired for heavy work, since he is thought of as a hard worker. One commercial man said that he would not take a *caboclo* as a clerk in his store for fear he would be cheated. Such expectations tend to direct people into certain occupations and to make it difficult for others to take other occupations.

Yet the most serious barrier to upward social mobility is not physical characteristics, but social position at birth. Movement from one of the lower strata into the 'first class' in Itá is extremely infrequent, no matter what the physical type of the lower-class man may be. Educational opportunities are almost totally lacking for the rural population, and the lower-class townspeople find it difficult to maintain their children in school for even the three-year course offered at the town school; only the relatively rich are able to send their children to the big city for further education. Economic improvement is likewise difficult. In Itá, the farmer uses antiquated methods which place a limit on his production; the rubber collector is caught between the prices paid for his product and the high prices which he pays for his necessities; and there is no industry or commerce to offer economic opportunity for the lower-class town-dweller.

Furthermore, should a member of the lower class, by some great fortune, improve his economic situation, he or she is faced with the necessity of learning new manners and new ways of behaving in order to move into the local upper class. He would also find the general knowledge of his lowly family origin a barrier. Usually, the only way for a person to rise in the social hierarchy is to move to another town.

The few cases of social ascension of which we were able to learn indicated that physical characteristics were perhaps less of a barrier

---

[1] A government publication states that as early as 1889, six of 14 commercial houses in Itá were owned by Hebrews. Such names as Aben Athar, Levi, Bensabeth and Azulay are mentioned. A synagogue was formed in Belém and Jewish families were found in small numbers in numerous small towns throughout the Valley. As in Itá, however, they no longer form a distinct group in the Amazon Valley. They are still known by their surnames but they have intermarried with Brazilians, and today most of them are Catholics and Brazilians. In Itá, their cemetery remains carefully watched over by Dona Deborah and is respected by the townspeople.

than the social factor. The best-known case was that of Lobato, the late husband of Dona Dora. He was the adopted son of Colonel Filomeno Cesar Andrade; his parents, who were Negroes, had left him as a small child in the care of this powerful commercial man. He was treated badly by his white foster father, and given menial tasks and manual labour to do. But he was an excellent worker and an astute trader. His foster father soon began to give him responsible tasks in the large store which he owned. Lobato married his foster-father's daughter, Dora, who was the child of her father's early union with a Negro common-law wife. It was thought by most people that the 'Colonel' would pass on his property to his two daughters by his legal wife who had been a *branca*, and that Dora and Lobato, her husband, would be ignored in his will. But, when the old man died, Lobato was given full charge of the store, and he knew more of his father-in-law's financial affairs than anyone else. It was Lobato who arranged the distribution of the Colonel's property, who received the largest share and who retained the business in Itá.

Lobato became the leading citizen of Itá, though he was a Negro, and his wife a dark *morena*. Colour was not a strong barrier to his success; his family backing, his commercial ability, his marriage to Dora and his economic success were sufficient to overcome any prejudice regarding his physical traits.

VI. Many of the attitudes and behaviour patterns in regard to race relations in Itá are common to most of Brazil: race or colour prejudice or discrimination is but one aspect of class prejudice and discrimination, and does not operate as a single factor determining the patterns of relationships between individuals or groups as it does for example in the United States. Social class is more important than racial type, and nowadays the two are no longer co-existent. A long period of miscegenation in Itá and in other Amazon communities has created a mixed population without creating racial sub-groups within the society. There are representatives of all possible physical types resulting from the mixture of three racial stocks in all social classes; one may say without any doubt that a race problem does not exist in Itá or in other small Amazon communities.

Yet there is still a class problem in Itá, as in most of rural Brazil. Social conditions have not been favourable to the ascension in the socio-economic hierarchy of the descendants of former slaves and of indentured 'semi-slaves'. Thus people of Indian and Negro physical type continue to hold an inferior social position. The physical characteristics of the Indian and the Negro, therefore, continue to be a symbol of low social rank, of descent from slaves or peons.

140

Yet some people of American Indian and Negro physical characteristics are nowadays members of the 'first class' of Itá and, in large cities of the Amazon Valley, members of the 'aristocracy'. While mobility between social classes remains in the Amazon relatively rigid, still there has been sufficient social ascension since colonial times to have made notable changes in the racial composition of these classes.

In one important way race relations in the Amazon area differ from those in other regions of Brazil. In the north-east coastal region, in the south, in the arid *sertão*—and in most of Brazil—the Indian was eliminated very early as an active element in the population; his lowly position in colonial society has been forgotten, and he has become a romantic figure which many aristocratic families feel proud to have in their genealogical tree. But in the Amazon few Africans were imported, and the Indian continued until the late nineteenth century to be the slave and the indentured labourer. The few Africans who did come were freemen, liberated in the plantation area of Negro slavery, or the highly valuable property of an aristocrat, to be treated with care and to be given superior tasks; it was the Indian who did the manual work and occupied the lowest position in colonial life. His descendants still have a low socio-economic position in Amazon society, and rank lower than the Negro. Just as the low social position of the Negro in other regions of Brazil results from his relatively recent slave status, the low position of the Amazon *caboclo* is a result of an original 'slave' status and an attitude of dispraisal toward the Indian which has persisted from the colonial era into the present.

BIBLIOGRAPHY

1. Correa Filho (1942), p. 283.
2. Bates, (1930), p. 282.
3. Wallace (1853), p. 479.
4. Agassiz (1896), p. 181.
5. Smith (1879), pp. 371—97.
6. Myrdal (1944), p. 39.
7. Ibid., p. 108.
8. Ibid., p. 39.
9. Koster (1816), p. 391.
10. Smith (1879), p. 118.
11. Delgado de Carvalho (1940), p. 238.

FROM CASTE TO CLASS IN NORTH BRAZIL

In 1500, before the Portuguese arrived in the New World, the population of the area of South America which is now Brazil consisted of approximately 1,500,000 Indians divided into numerous linguistic and tribal groups. There was no unity among these peoples; instead each tribe, sometimes each village, lived in a state of intense suspicion of its neighbours. Warfare was almost continuous between many tribes, and the native population did not offer any unified resistance to the Portuguese newcomers. After 1500, there was a rapid disintegration of organized Indian society under the constant pressure of the aggressive Europeans.

The Portuguese did not come to Brazil to work. At first they were content to trade with the Indians for Brazilwood, but they soon turned to enslaving the native peoples in order to secure labour to make gardens which would provide them with food and to perform other tasks. Expeditions were organized to penetrate into the interior to capture Indian slaves. Despite the constant efforts of the Jesuits and other religious orders to protect the Indians from the slave-hungry colonists, and despite the laws promulgated by the Portuguese Crown against Indian slavery, the colonists continued to make slaves of the aboriginal peoples throughout the first two centuries of Brazilian history. The originally sparse aboriginal population was thus drastically reduced by slavery, by the wars made upon them by the Portuguese, and by European diseases against which they had no specific immunity. Whole tribes migrated inland to escape the ravages of the Portuguese and, by 1750, few Indians remained in the coastal fringe which was the effective area of the Portuguese colony.

It was soon apparent to the European, especially after the introduction of sugar cane in the middle of the sixteenth century, that they must look elsewhere for slaves. As early as 1538 the first African slaves were imported into Brazil. A period which lasted over 200 years began, during which there was a steady flow of Negroes across the Atlantic to Brazil. A very conservative estimate has it that approximately 3,300,000 Negro slaves entered Brazil in the seventeenth and eighteenth centuries alone, but the number was probably greater [2][1]. For a time, during the colonial period, there were more African slaves in Brazil than Europeans.

Brazil was founded as a society formed of two distinct castes[2]—

---

[1] The figures in brackets refer to the bibliography on page 155.

[2] The term 'caste' is used in the sense that it is used by North American sociologists to describe 'Negro-white' relations in the United States. 'Caste' is used thus for an endogamous and hereditary group which in the two cases (i.e., North America and early colonial Brazil) were made up of racial groups. See Gunnar Myrdal, *An American Dilemma* (New York, 1944), pp. 667-69, and John Dollard, *Caste and Class in a Southern Town* (New Haven, 1937).

namely, a caste of European masters and a caste of Indian or Negro slaves. Brazilian society, however, consisted exclusively of castes for only a very short time. Intermediate social groups began to take form almost immediately after 1500. In fact, when the Portuguese arrived to settle in Salvador (Bahia), which was one of the first settlements along the coast, they found Indian half-breeds. The famous Caramurú (Diego Alvares Correia), a Portuguese sailor who had probably been left there by a French boat as early as 1509-11, was found living with his numerous children by various Indian women[2]. Very few Portuguese women came to Brazil in the first days of the colony, and the Portuguese men are said to have found the Indian women exceedingly attractive. Miscegenation between Portuguese males and Indian women began almost at once; the *mamelucos*, the offspring of these unions, were raised as freemen and the European whites took wives from among the half-breed and quarter-breed women. A group of European-Indian *mestiços* were formed who stood midway between the European *élite* and the Indian slaves.

Race mixture continued with ever-increasing speed after the arrival of African slaves in large numbers. The Portuguese plantation owners, their sons and relatives took concubines from among the Negro slaves and the sons of these white fathers and Negro mothers were often given special treatment. They were taught to be administrators on plantations; they were made freemen; and they were often educated—a few were even sent to Portugal, where they attended the famous University of Coimbra. Soon mulattoes were represented among the professional classes as lawyers and physicians, they entered the priesthood and public life[3], and not only mulattoes but also Negroes gained their liberty and entered the economic and public life of the Colony during slave times. As Frank Tannenbaum has shown in his excellent essay entitled *Slave and Citizen* [4], one of the characteristics of slavery in Latin America which distinguished it from slavery in the English colonies and in the United States was the numerous methods provided in Latin America for manumission. By 1798 there were 406,000 free Negroes living in Brazil, and by the time of abolition in 1888 it is estimated that there were three times as many Negro freemen as Negro slaves [5]. These freemen—Negroes, mulattoes, and others of part Negro descent—formed a series of social strata between the European slave-owning caste and the lowly slaves.

Almost at once the relations between the Portuguese masters and their Indian and Negro slaves began to produce intermediary social strata between the two castes. By the end of slavery, the intermediate freeman class made up of people of Negroid, Indian and Caucasian racial stocks, and of a wide variety of *mestiços*, was numerically more important than the white *élite* or the Negro slaves. With abolition in

143

1888 the slaves entered Brazilian society as freemen, although at the bottom of the social hierarchy. Then in the late nineteenth and early twentieth centuries a relatively large number of European workers entered the country to join the ex-slaves and low-class freemen as labourers on plantations and in industry. Meantime, many land-holding families of 'pure' European descent lost their aristocratic status and their dominant political position as they became less wealthy or even impoverished; many aristocrats have dropped in social status from the 'white *élite* caste' to the level of the people who were descendants of slaves. Simultaneously, individuals who were descendants of slaves or low-class freemen have improved their economic and social standing; people of mixed racial ancestry and descendants of recent European immigrants have so prospered that they are represented among the financial and politically dominating class of the country. Especially since the formation of the Republic, politics has offered a road to social advancement, and many Bra-zilian families now of high rank first came to the fore during the early Republic; the 'old families' of colonial aristocrats have inter-married with this new upper class, and the old European caste has been broken down throughout most of the country. *Where Brazilian society was once formed by castes, it has now become a society of social classes which are themselves undergoing rapid change.*

Class lines are still rigidly drawn in Brazil. The descendants of the old white aristocracy with the new upper class which results from new fortunes and from relatively recent political success, form a small upper class which maintains many of the ideals of the old slave-owning aristocratic caste. These people follow a comfortable, even luxurious, way of life with all the educational advantages, the forms of recreation, and the technological equipment available to the economically well-off in any modern Western country. There is, however, a rapidly expanding middle class which is comprised of government employees, professional groups, commercial and indus-trial employees, owners of small business enterprises, and so on. The members of this Brazilian middle class generally identify themselves with the upper class, sharing to a great extent in their 'aristocratic' values and ideals, and follow an upper-class pattern of life so far as their smaller incomes allow. They differ thus from the middle class of other Western countries which forms the numerical backbone of the nation and is proud of its values and way of life. Finally, in modern Brazil there is a large 'lower class', mostly il-literate, whose miserable standard of living offers a striking con-trast to that of the contemporary upper class, even to that of the growing middle class. It is composed of the many subsistence farmers throughout the country, the workers on plantations, the industrial workers, the domestic servants, and the innumerable groups of people who perform manual labour of all sorts.

144

The numerical importance of these three contemporary social classes is difficult to estimate with precision. A study made of Brazilian national income a few years back, however, provides us with a basis for an estimate. According to Dr. Henry W. Spiegel, in 1944 a total of only 300,000 people, comprising only 2.5 per cent of those gainfully employed, received 30 per cent of the total national income, and another 2.5 per cent received 20 per cent. Thus, 5 per cent of those gainfully employed received 50 per cent of the national income; in economic terms, this 5 per cent represents the upper class. Urban workers contributing to the various social insurance organizations formed 24 per cent of those gainfully employed, but received only 20 per cent of the national income; although numerous groups are excluded from this figure, this seems to represent the situation and numerical importance of the middle class in modern Brazilian society. The agriculturalists (the small farmer, the share-cropper, the agricultural wage-earner) made up no less than 71 per cent of those gainfully employed and yet received only 30 per cent of the national income [6]. These latter, plus numerous others whose incomes are so insignificant that they are never recorded, make up the great lower class of modern Brazil.

Unfortunately, there are no similar studies which might allow us to estimate accurately the racial composition of these nation-wide class groups. However, most Brazilians and most foreign students of Brazil wonder that the upper class is composed almost exclusively of European whites or people 'in whom the traces of Indian or Negro blood are infinitesimal' [7]. The middle class is also predominantly Caucasoid, though numerous *mestiços* of various racial backgrounds have been able to ascend into this group. It is in the lower classes that the large mass of Negroes, of mulattoes, of people with American Indian characteristics, and of *pardos* (the convenient Brazilian term meaning 'brown' which is used for people of all racial mixtures) are found. Although a process of 'bleaching'—or progressive tendency of the Brazilian population toward a generalized Caucasoid appearance—is probably taking place, the homogeneous 'Brazilian race' predicted by many authors is still in the future. Today, class lines generally divide the more Caucasoid Brazilians from those who might be called 'people of colour'. As yet, economic opportunities and educational advantages have not been extended to the rural masses nor even to all the urban poor; thus, the majority of the 'people of colour' remain in the lower class. *It is thus still a general rule throughout Brazil that the people of the upper class are almost exclusively Caucasian in appearance, and the majority of the 'people of colour' are found in the middle and lower classes.*

In the rural communities which have been described in this report, a shift from a caste society to a society based upon social classes has taken place, it has throughout the country. But the class system has not suffered the more recent influences of industrialization, of modern ideology, and of other innovations to the degree that other parts of Brazil have felt them. More is retained of the nineteenth century in these communities than in the large metropolitan centres on the coast.

All the social classes of a nation are never, of course, present in any one local community, and those described in the four rural com-

TABLE I. Brazilian social classes: in the community and in the Nation

National	Vila Recôncavo	Minas Velhas	Monte Serrat	Itá
Upper class	Aristocrats	Not present *Brancos-Ricos*	Not present 'Os Bons'	Not present
Middle class	Local upper class	(white-rich) Class A -------------- Class B 1	(big shots) Class I -------------- Class II A	'First Class' or 'Os Brancos' (the whites)
Lower class	Local middle class	*Preto-Pobre* (negro-poor) Class B 2	'Os Pobres' (the poor) Class II B	'Second Class' (lower class town-dwellers) -------------- 'Farmers' (Rural lower class)
	Local lower class	Class C	Class III	'Collectors' (rural lower class)

N.B. The dotted lines represent social cleavages between important segments of a social class; the solid lines cleavages between social classes. Although the term 'class' has been used by Hutchinson, Harris and Zimmerman to describe important social and economic segments of the prestige and status hierarchy of the communities under study, it is agreed that on the basis of multiple criteria for class placement Minas Velhas, Monte Serrat, and Itá are two-class societies, and that Vila Recôncavo has but three classes when considered in the broader perspective of the region or the nation. The functionally important classification of people as *branco-rico-preto-pobre* (Minas Velhas) or as *os Bons-os Pobres* (Monte Serrat) cuts across important social and economic groups present in each community. As each author has shown, however, it is this cleavage which is important in these communities in determining status and personal relations.

munities of our study represent only a segment of the social strata present in the nation as a whole; yet they may be equated in a general way with those of the nation. Since all these communities are relatively isolated and are situated in agricultural areas, analogous social classes may be with one exception found in all four communities. The approximate relationship of the social classes in the four communities may be equated with those of the nation and with one another as shown in Table I.

Only in the sugar-producing region of the Bahian Recôncavo are there representatives of the national upper class. In the community of Vila Recôncavo, sugar-producing has continued to provide an adequate profit since the early seventeenth century. Despite many fluctuations of price and despite the blow of abolition, the old landowning aristocrats have been able to maintain their hold on numerous plantations. Today, their existence is being theatened by large corporations which are establishing modern sugar mills in the area and purchasing plantations; but in turn the directors of these corporations, who are frequently of the new upper class deriving from political and financial success, tend to identify themselves with and to marry into the old plantation families.

The old aristocrats have disappeared from Minas Velhas and Itá, and may never have existed in Monte Serrat. There was a time in the past, however, when each of these communities had a traditionally wealthy class. When mining was a more lucrative enterprise, during the eighteenth and early nineteenth centuries, Minas Velhas was the centre of a prosperous aristocratic class the members of which, although perhaps not as socially acceptable or as powerful politically as the sugar aristocrats on the coast, certainly belonged to the national upper class. During the period when there were enormous ranches in the *sertão*, some people were wealthy and well-educated enough to be recognized in the coastal cities as 'traditional families' of the upper class. Even the small town of Itá had members of the regional and national aristocracy during the great rubber boom. There was a 'Baron of Itá', a title granted by the Emperor Pedro II, and the wealthy rubber traders were recognized in the large city of Belém as people of importance in the region. In Minas Velhas and Itá, however, as the basis of their wealth disappeared members of upper-class families moved away, seeking to maintain their standard of living elsewhere and by other means. The individuals of this class who remained have been forced to stay and to earn their living as others in the community and have, so to speak, 'lost caste'—lost their identity as a separate aristocratic group. This process was an important one; it has produced in three communities of our study— and in numerous others like them throughout rural Brazil—a less rigid class system than existed before, and one in which economic, educational and personal factors more often provide the means of social advancement. The absence of the old aristocratic caste in these communities has led to greater social mobility—to a local society without any absolute barriers to upward social ascension.

The 'local upper class' of Vila Recôncavo, the *'brancos ricos'* of Minas Velhas, *'os bons'* of Monte Serrat, and the first class (or *'os brancos'*) of Itá are, in each case, the local representatives of the national middle class. In lieu of the national upper class, these groups form the upper social and economic strata of the local com-

147

munity. The 'local upper class' is a rapidly-growing group in rural Brazil including federal, State, and municipal employees, small landowners, business people, and professionals of all kinds. It is into this class that people of the lower class rise when they become educated or improve their economic condition; and it is in this class also that the competition for relative social rank is most intense.

Likewise, the lower classes of all four communities are generally equivalent to each other and to the lower class of the nation as a whole. Their occupations differ somewhat, although the small subsistence farmer is present in all four communities; in Itá there are rubber collectors; in Minas Velhas, artisans; in Vila Recôncavo, labourers on the sugar plantations, workers in the mill, and fishermen; and in Monte Serrat, *vaqueiros* (cowboys) and a few artisans. Everywhere this class is made up of people who do manual labour. Everywhere these people, like the industrial and manual workers of the cities, have a low standard of living.

The composition of these social classes in the four communities gives us important clues as to the nature of race relations in rural Brazil. First, the 'aristocrats' of Vila Recôncavo contain not a single individual who is not Caucasian in physical appearance or who is known to have Negroid ancestors. This class, as stated earlier, is almost national in scope and has been enlarged by the addition of people who have been successful financially and politically in the recent past. With the addition of these people to the upper class, individuals who are known to have a Negro ancestor have been accepted by the aristocrats in other communities and in big cities; even members of the old aristocracy, such as those found in Vila Recôncavo, claim Indian ancestors in the distant past. But in the experience of the authors, there are no members of this class who are Negroid in appearance or who are even dark *mestiços*, although there have been exceptions to this rule in the past, and there must be a few exceptions even today. *With rare exceptions, the people of the upper class of Brazil are Caucasian in physical appearance.*

In the four communities studied the 'local upper class' groups, representing the national middle class, are also predominantly white in physical appearance. But numerous people of mixed ancestry have entered these groups, and there are many cases of people with both Indian and Negroid physical appearance who are classed as upper-class in local terms. The people who make up these local upper-class groups are generally those who have climbed socially and economically, and it is noteworthy that fewer Negroes and dark *mestiços* have achieved this position than whites. The criteria for placing an individual in this group are numerous and vary somewhat from community to community; but *it may be said that in all the communities studied one's income, the kind of work one does, one's education, one's family (in varying degrees), and finally, one's physical appearance, are*

148

the main criteria used. The individuals of each community might be graded in a separate prestige series according to each of these criteria, but the social position of any individual in the community derives from the total effect of all these principal criteria as well as from others which are less important and sometimes local in scope. Thus a man might be poor, but have a white collar job, a secondary education, be a descendant of a locally well-known family, be Caucasian in physical appearance and be placed in the local upper class; or he might be a Negro but have the other qualifications for membership in the local upper class and be so classified. These criteria for class are given different value—or different weight, so to speak—in the various communities; thus racial characteristics seem to have greater importance in Minas Velhas than in the other three communities studied, and a Negro who has all other qualifications is excluded from the upper stratum simply because he is a Negro. The position of an individual according to each of these criteria of rank tends in general to be more or less compatible; a person is white, has a good income according to local standards, has a 'white collar' job, and comes of a 'good family'. *But since competition for membership in this local upper class, and the competition for social ranking within it, is relatively intense, it is at this point in the social hierarchy that the criterion of race becomes most crucial in determining social position.* If and when tension exists between people of these communities because of 'race', it is between people striving to enter the local upper class who are competing for relative position within the class.

The lower-class groups in all four communities, as throughout Brazil, contain people of all racial types. Among these people, racial type is also a criterion for relative social rank within their class. In actual personal relationships, however, racial characteristics seem to be of little importance, being overshadowed by income, occupation, and other criteria both personal and social; though the existence of preferences as to racial type and even of derogatory attitudes toward people of different racial characteristics within this lower group does indicate that *a mild form of racial prejudice exists on all levels of society in rural Brazil.* But the lack of emphasis upon race within the lower class also indicates that this prejudice is so to speak latent, only becoming active when competition for the upper positions of the local social hierarchy is involved. That the majority of the 'people of colour' in all four communities belong to the lower-class groups reflects the well-known fact about Brazil that, in the relatively short period since the end of slavery, opportunity for social advancement through education and economic improvement has not been provided for the descendants of ex-slaves. Negroid physical characteristics (and in the Amazon those of the Indian as well) are symbols of slave ancestry, and such people still have jobs involving manual labour in one form or another, which is another

149

sign of low status since it was the slave in the past who did such work. Lack of education, the performance of manual labour, a low income, absence of family backing, and racial type, are all at work together to keep the 'people of colour' in the lower rungs of society.

Yet, in these rural communities of north Brazil, this prejudice is mainly one of social class rather than one directly focused upon people having a particular set of racial characteristics.[1] Except in Vila Recôncavo, where the landowning aristocratic white caste persists, there are no positions in these rural societies closed to an individual because of 'race'. Despite the derogatory stereotypes expressed in each community regarding the Negro (and in Itá regarding the American Indian physical type also), the actual behaviour toward people of those physical types differs strikingly from the attitude as verbally expressed; actual interpersonal relations seem to be determined by other factors such as wealth, education, personal attachments and political position, rather than 'race'.[2]

Furthermore, actual physical segregation of people according to physical type (except in the satellite villages of Minas Velhas—see below) is absent. Segregation of people of any 'racial' type in schools, residential districts, public buildings, or in other ways so common in North America and South Africa and some other parts of the world, is unthinkable to the people of these communities. The idea that people should be excluded from the right to vote because of 'racial' type strikes most people as rather comical. That there should even be laws in some parts of the world which prohibit marriage between people of different racial groups would puzzle the people of these Brazilian communities profoundly. Never in the history of any of these communities, to our knowledge, has there since slave times been any violence resulting from tensions between people of different racial type.

Likewise, there are no organizations of Negroes or people of Indian physical type which are limited to people of that 'racial' group. The Sociedade dos Pobres of Minas Velhas, although containing many Negroes and many dark *mestiços*, also contains people of other physical types, and its very name indicates that 'being poor' is the qualification for membership. In Itá, the Brotherhood of St. Benedict was made up mainly of Negroes and led by the 'old Negroes' but, like most Brazilian organizations founded on a basis of 'race', the membership soon came to be representative of a wide range of racial types in the community.[3] In these rural societies, there are no associations based exclusively upon racial differences. In these communities, it is as people say throughout Brazil: 'We are

[1] Pierson compares this prejudice to that existing within the Negro caste in the United States (*Negroes in Brazil*, Chicago, 1942, p. 341).

[2] As a recent North American visitor to Brazil exclaimed: 'Brazilians say they have race prejudice but act without it; we sometimes say we are free of it but our prejudice shows in our actions.'

[3] In a recent Congresso Nacional do Negro held in Rio de Janeiro to consider the position of the Negro

all Brazilians' (*somos todos brasileiros*). The Brazilian Negroes do not attempt to improve their social and economic position as a group, but as members of lower class and as individuals who are members of one society.

In a generally similar picture of race and class relations, each of the communities described in this report shows however certain variations. Of the four communities, Minas Velhas stands out as the one where prejudice, even discrimination, takes its strongest form. In the two satellite villages of Minas Velhas, residential segregation actually occurs and the force of the derogatory attitudes against the Negro, even overt exclusion of Negroes from the Social Club, shows 'race' as a strong factor in determining social position there. This situation may be due to the nature of modern economic adaptation in Minas Velhas, and also to the form of slave-master relationship which existed in that region. The slaves who worked in the mines did not have the close and intimate relations with the master which were possible on the plantations. The owners were often suspicious of their slaves, who they feared might secrete and sell precious stones. This was hardly conducive to warm relations between the two castes. Following the collapse of the mining industry and after abolition, the formation of an artisan class in Minas Velhas led to the social and economic ascension of numerous descendants of slaves; there was a simultaneous loss of social position (or exodus) of the mine-owning class. People of Negro and mixed ancestry rose to compete with the whites for social and economic position. In Minas Velhas, this led to the formation of a set of interpersonal relations and to attitudes toward people of Negroid stock which, compared to those in the other communities studied, are antagonistic and rigid.

In Vila Recôncavo, many of the patterns of race relations which must have existed on the sugar plantations along the north-east coast in the nineteenth century still persist. The plantation workers are usually Negroes, and the plantation owners mostly white. The artisans, the specialized workers in the mills and on the plantations, and the various special groups in the town are frequently of mixed ancestry. Although there is still a great social distance between the white aristocracy and the Negro workers, and even between the local upper class and the lower strata, relations between the racial groups and between social classes are tempered by the continuance of good personal relations between individuals. Despite the nearness of Vila Recôncavo to the large city of Salvador, it has changed less in this way than any of the other communities described. It is a society in which the Negro worker, the mulatto artisan or town-dweller, and

in Brazil, there were complaints by Negroes of the number of whites and mulattoes who seemed to be taking the leadership in the Congress. The Sociedade dos Homens de Côr (Society of Men of Colour), with headquarters in Rio de Janeiro, has never appealed to a large membership. Numerous organizations of Negroes have appeared in Rio de Janeiro, but most of them have had a short life. See Pierson, op. cit., pp. 342-43.

the white upper class are fully aware of their obligations and rights. In other words, everyone knows his or her place. There is thus relatively little competition for social position, and Vila Recôncavo seems to have less tension between social classes and racial groups than the other communities.

In Monte Serrat the people are, on the whole, more homogeneous in physical appearance than those of Minas Velhas, Vila Recôncavo, and Itá, although individuals of all physical types are present. The percentage of Negroes is negligible and, though there are a number of people who are basically Caucasoid in appearance, the majority are of the *caboclo* type (mixed Indian ancestry). In addition, Monte Serrat, unlike the other communities, has never been the scene of a major Brazilian boom. Social and economic differences are noticeable, as they are in almost any rural community of north Brazil, but the majority of the people have a roughly similar standard of living and way of life. This fact is reflected in race relations, and in the relations between the social classes, which are neither as antagonistic as in Minas Velhas or as fixed and personalized as in Vila Recôncavo. Monte Serrat represents a case of but mild racial prejudice and of relatively fluid social classes and as such is characteristic of numerous rural communities throughout north Brazil.

The Amazon community of Itá has certain characteristics unique in Brazil. The Amazon is a backward and isolated part of the country, more so than the regions in which the other three communities described in this report are situated. After the rubber collapse in 1912, it was almost forgotten by the nation until very recently. The American Indian has figured much more largely in the historical background of the Amazon than elsewhere; he was the slave, and the few Negroes who came to the valley were most of them already freemen. Thus, the race situation in Itá is marked by the low position awarded the descendant of the Indian and the comparatively high prestige attached to Negro ancestry, although, as everywhere, the Caucasian or white is given the highest place. Itá is the smallest of the four communities, the poorest and the least influenced by modern trends. In this community dark mulattoes are full-fledged members of the highest rungs of the local upper class, and in the recent past, the man of highest prestige was a Negro. In Itá the process of race mixture and the breakdown of the old colonial social structure has taken place slowly and unaffected by the recent social and economic changes spreading from urban Brazil.

Finally, it should be said that the hypotheses set forth by Donald Pierson in the conclusions of his study of race relations in Salvador are generally reaffirmed by these studies of race and class relations in rural north Brazil. Among the more important of these hypotheses are: (a) that Brazil is a multiracial class society 'distinct from Indian, for example, where the social order is based upon the principle of caste and from those parts of the world where a national or racial minority (or minorities) is in free association with, but not accepted by, a dominant national or racial majority...'[8]; (b) 'Prejudice exists in Brazil; but it is *class* rather than *race* prejudice'[9]; (c) 'This does not mean that there are no social distinctions in Brazil.... Neither does it mean that there is no discrimination or that blacks or mixed bloods are completely satisfied with their lot. But it does mean (a) that a man of colour may, by reason of individual merit or favourable circumstances, improve his status and even achieve position in the upper levels of society and (b) that this position will then be with reference not merely to the darker group whose colour he shares but to the total community' [10]. Thus Pierson's study, which had reference primarily to the city of Salvador in Bahia, seems to hold true generally for a wide area of the rural north.

On the other hand, certain additions to Pierson's hypotheses seem to be suggested by the four studies here. These might be stated as follows:

1. In some communities of north Brazil, a remnant of a white aristocratic caste is found, membership of which is closed to the Negro, the dark *mestiço*, and even those who have Negro ancestry or marked Negroid features.

2. In both the cities and the rural communities of north Brazil, there is a decided preference for Caucasian physical features. People of mixed ancestry are considered physically attractive and, in fact, the *'morena'* is the ideal feminine beauty[11], but the features of these mixed-blood beauties which are emphasized are mainly Caucasian, with the exception of their darker skin.

3. The common Brazilian statement that 'We Brazilians are becoming one people' seems to imply that Brazilians hope to become a nation more Caucasian in physical appearance. The process of absorption of the Negro into the white population discussed by Pierson, and the 'bleaching' process mentioned by T. Lynn Smith, are both part of the unstated race policy of Brazil [12].

4. In the city of Salvador as in the rural communities studied, the Negro is considered the best worker (meaning in general, the most capable at manual labour), which is a rather doubtful compliment in view of the attitude of most Brazilians toward manual labour. Negro physical characteristics are universally considered ugly.

5. The attitude toward people of American Indian ancestry varies widely, depending upon the historical role of the Indian in the local scene. Among the aristocrats of the city and of the rural districts, Indian ancestors in the distant past are proof of a long Brazilian genealogy and thus a point of pride. But, in the Amazon, the attitude toward the *caboclo* reflects the former slave status of the Indian.

6. In rural north Brazil, people are acutely conscious of physical

153

race. This is shown by the numerous categories of racial types used in all the communities studied. This consciousness of physical race is not related to discrimination, as it is in other countries. On the contrary, it is in Brazil (a) a system by which individuals are described; (b) a way of diagnosing a person's probable social rank, and (c) a mechanism by which 'people of colour' can avoid the stigma of being classed as Negroes.

7. The expression of prejudice against the Negroes, the *mestiços* and people of Indian physical type is mainly manifested verbally and not in behaviour. Other factors (wealth, occupation, education, etc.) are of greater importance in determining the actual patterns of inter-personal relations than race.

8. Although rural Brazilian society has a rigid class structure, conflict between social classes is relatively subdued. Instead, individuals strive to improve their status by moving—as individuals—into an upper class, without questioning the principle of the existing system of social classes.

9. Finally, the ability of 'people of colour' to improve their status in rural Brazil varies considerably from community to community according to the possibilities open to them; everywhere it depends upon improving their educational level, their occupation, their economic situation, and their family connexions—factors which, combined with their physical type, give people their social position.

The system of inter-racial relations which has taken form in Brazil, with all its faults and its advantages, provides a comparatively favourable and fertile basis for the future growth of Brazilian society. Brazil has taken the form of a multi-racial society unlike that found in most colonial areas of the world where a rigid 'colour line' is usual.[13] In most colonial areas, the intense and emotionally charged feelings of the native population (generally of Mongoloid or Negroid racial stock) toward the dominant European 'caste', and the clash of economic interests between the racial castes, create numerous barriers to the improvement of social and economic conditions. Brazil has avoided developing a caste society such as that of the United States, where the strict line between the Negro and the white has been such a costly drain upon the nation and the individual. With the rapid economic development of Brazil, which is now under way, there should be more numerous opportunities for individuals to improve their economic status throughout the country, and Brazil should be able to make educational facilities available to its people on a much broader basis than at present. As the standard of living and the educational level of the lower strata of Brazilian society improve, the people of darker skin colour now occupying the lower ranks should take their place in the middle ranks of society. There are no serious racial barriers to social and economic advance and, as opportunities increase, larger numbers of people will rise in the social system. The great contrasts in social and economic conditions between the darker lower strata and the predominantly white upper class should disappear.

There are dangers, however, along the road to this ideal. There are indications both in the present studies and in reports from the great metropolitan centres of the country that discrimination, tensions, and prejudices based on race are appearing. As has been pointed out [14], when the number of individuals of Negro or mixed ancestry improve their educational and economic position, they challenge the dominant position of the white upper class. This might well result in emphasis upon 'race' as a criterion for social position, in greater prejudice, in tension between racial groups, and even in discrimination. Furthermore, as Brazil becomes more closely tied to the Western industrial and commercial world, and develops its technological equipment, it will be exposed to the ideology of the more industrialized and technologically developed nations. The borrowing of cultural elements—of instruments, techniques, and concepts—is not a mechanical process. There is a tendency for new elements to be diffused from one culture to another in complexes or in clusters; attitudes, ideas, and even material objects often pass from one culture to another somewhat as appendages of a desired innovation. Both Brazilians and foreign observers have the impression that Western attitudes and concepts of racism are entering Brazil along with industrial and technological improvements. But there is no inherent relationship between Western industrialism and technology and Western racism, no necessary connexion between the widespread improvement of social conditions and the development, through competition, of tensions and discrimination between racial or minority groups. Aware of the dangers and pitfalls and taking care to avoid them, Brazil may enjoy the benefits of technological change, and of greater rewards for its underdeveloped potentialities, without losing its rich heritage of racial democracy.

BIBLIOGRAPHY

1. Ramos (1944), p. 119.
2. Azevedo (1949), p. 64 ff.
3. See Pierson (1942), Ch. VI, and Freyre (1946), especially Ch. V.
4. New York, 1947.
5. Ramos, op. cit., p. 119.
6. 'Income, Savings, and Investment in Brazil', *Inter-American Economic Affairs*, Vol. I, No. 1 (June 1947), p. 116 ff.
7. Smith (1946), p. 174.
8. Pierson, op. cit., p. 348.

9. Ibid., p. 349.
10. Ibid., p. 349. A complete list of Pierson's concluding hypotheses may be found on pp. 344-50.
11. Ibid., p. 136.
12. Ibid., p. 125 ff., and Smith, op. cit., p. 173 ff.
13. Kennedy (1945), p. 308.
14. See Harris, *infra*, p. 47.

BIBLIOGRAPHY

AZEVEDO, Thales de. *Povoamento da Cidade do Salvador*, Bahia. 1949.

BUARQUE DE HOLANDA, Sergio. *Raizes do Brasil*, 2nd edition; Rio de Janeiro. 1948.

BATES, Henry Walter. *The Naturalist on the River Amazon*, Everyman Library, London. 1930.

BILDEN, Rudiger. 'Brazil, Laboratory of Civilization', *The Nation*, Vol. 128, 16 January. 1929.

CALMON, Pedro. *Historia da Civilização Brasileira*, 2nd edition, São Paulo. 1935.

CARNEIRO, Edison. *Candomblés da Bahia*, Publicações do Museu do Estado, No. 8, Bahia. 1948.

CORRÊA FILHO, Virgilio. 'Devassamento e Ocupação da Amazônia Brasileira', *Revista Brasileira de Geografia*, Vol. IV, No. 2. 1942.

CUNHA, Euclides da. *Revolt in the Backlands*, Translated by Samuel Putnam, University of Chicago. 1944.

DELGADO DE CARVALHO, Carlos. 'Lectures on Brazilian Affairs', *The Rice Institute Pamphlet*, Vol. XXVII, No. 4. 1940.

DOLLARD, John. *Caste and Class in a Southern Town*, New Haven. 1937.

DIÊGUES JUNIÓR, Manuel. *O Bangue nas Alagôas*, Rio de Janeiro. 1949.

FREYRE, Gilberto. *Brazil: An Interpretation*, New York. 1945.

——. *The Masters and the Slaves*, Translated by Samuel Putnam, New York. 1946.

JAMES, Preston. *Latin America*, New York. 1942.

——. *Brazil*, New York. 1946.

——. 'The São Francisco Basin: A Brazilian Sertão', *The Geographical Review*, Vol. 38, No. 4, pp. 658-61.

KENNEDY, Raymond. 'The Colonial Crisis and the Future', *The Science of Man in the World Crisis*, Edited by Ralph Linton, New York. 1945.

KOSTER, Henry. *Travels in Brazil*, London. 1816.

LANDIS, Ruth. *City of Women*, New York. 1947.

LIMA JUNIOR, Augusto. *História dos Diamantes nas Minas Gerais*, Rio de Janeiro. 1945.

MARCHANT, Alexander. *From Barter to Slavery*, The Johns Hopkins University Studies in Historical and Political Science, Vol. LX, Baltimore. 1942.

MYRDAL, Gunnar. *An American Dilemma*, New York. 1944.

157

OLIVEIRA MARTINS, J. F. *O Brasil e as Colônias Portuguêsas*, 3rd edition, Lisbon. 1880.

PIERSON, Donald. *Negroes in Brazil: A study of Race Contact in Bahia*, Chicago. 1942.

RAMOS, Artur. *O Negro Brasileiro*, São Paulo. 1934.

RAMOS, Artur. *Las Poblaciones del Brasil*, Mexico D.F. 1944.

RODRIGUES, Nina. *Os Africanos no Brasil*, São Paulo. 1935.

SMITH, Herbert H. *Brazil: The Amazons and the Coast*, New York. 1879.

SMITH, T. Lynn. *Brazil: People and Institutions*, Baton Rouge, 1946.

SMITH, T. Lynn and MARCHANT, Alexander, editors. *Brazil: Portrait of a Half Continent*, New York, 1951.

SPIEGEL, Henry W. 'Income, Savings, and Investment in Brazil', *Inter-American Economic Affairs*, Vol. I, No. 1, 1947.

TANNENBAUM, Frank. *Slave and Citizen*, New York, 1947.

WAGLEY, Charles. 'Brazil', Most of the World, Edited by Ralph Linton, New York, 1949.

WALLACE, Alfred Russel. *Narratives and Travels in the Amazon and Rio Negro*, London, 1853.

WANDERLEY DE ARAUJO PINHO, José. *Testamento de Mem Sá*, Rio de Janeiro, 1941.

ZARUR, Jorge. *A Bacia do Médio São Francisco*, Rio de Janeiro, 1947.